Pierre Henri Treyssac de Vergy

Henrietta, Countess Osenvor

A Sentimental Novel in a series of Letters to Lady Susannah Fitzroy

Pierre Henri Treyssac de Vergy

Henrietta, Countess Osenvor

A Sentimental Novel in a series of Letters to Lady Susannah Fitzroy

ISBN/EAN: 9783337039561

Printed in Europe, USA, Canada, Australia, Japan

Cover: Foto ©ninafisch / pixelio.de

More available books at **www.hansebooks.com**

A

SENTIMENTAL NOVEL.

IN A

SERIES OF LETTERS

TO

LADY SUSANNAH FITZROY,

BY MR. TREYSSAC DE VERGY,

COUNSELLOR IN THE PARLIAMENT OF PARIS.

IN TWO VOLUMES.

" LOVE AND VIRTUE HELD THE PEN."

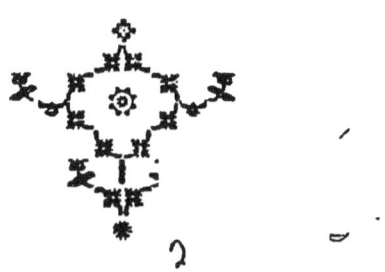

LONDON:
Printed for HARRISON and Co. No. 18, Paternoster Row.
M DCC LXXXV.

TO

LADY HARRIET STANHOPE.

MADAM,

WERE Virtue, Beauty, and the Graces, to appear among us, they would assume your shape, your features—talk and feel as you do.

I am,

Madam,

Your Ladyship's

Most humble and

Obedient Servant,

TREYSSAC DE VERGY.

PREFACE.

OF my former works Love and Nature were the authors; they boldly held the pencil, and drew the pictures of the Lovers. The drapery intended to conceal their voluptuousness making them the more conspicuous, a few fools arose against the performance, and announced it as an apology for adultery. As I despised their judgment, I appealed only to my own reason, and sat contented with the esteem of the sensible, and laughing heartily at the noisy buzzing of the harmless insects.

Henrietta Virtue has written; and I doubt not but for that very reason it will be damned. Men judging according to their age and passions, I wonder not at the praise and satire lavished by them on the same work. A woman, as she smiles or frowns, partakes of it's fate; like it, she has her censors and admirers: no more than she do I pretend to please all; too well am I acquainted with the human heart to indulge the idle, flattering conceit. As we feel, we see and read; the gay and passionate, the devotee and indifferent, having a soul the reverse of each other, must necessarily differ in their opinion of a beauty and a novel.

Of Henrietta I will say but this: all the characters are new. If good, the publick will do it justice; if bad, to commend it would be ridiculous.

HENRIETTA.

HENRIETTA,

COUNTESS OSENVOR.

VOLUME THE FIRST.

LETTER I.

HENRIETTA COUNTESS OSENVOR, TO LADY SUSANNAH FITZROY.

TOO cruel Susannah! Did you know the full extent of my misery, your curiosity would die away, and respect my sorrow! You would not attempt to renew in my heart a pain too exquisite to be borne! Oh, let me not call the past to my mind! my soul sinks at the remembrance of it. Five years are elapsed, it is true: time has no power over sufferings like mine; it may have blunted their former fierceness; but they are still keen, still intolerable; I have no strength to support them. You say I pine away. I know it. What is life when deprived of the only charm which could make it agreeable! Would I were no more! That at this very moment death would sweep me away! Religion stops my arm; nay, your friendship is a comfort: I enjoy in the midst of grief, trouble, and despair. When I see you, I am less unhappy. You are, to me, like a fine day to the dispirited seamen, after a night of storm; you enliven my spirits, and sometimes force a smile on my lips: but, when absent, memory betrays me again into the feeling of my wretchedness; I have then no other company than my thoughts, and these thoughts are a perpetual torment.

Susannah! insist no more to know a secret which must be buried with me in the grave! it would be too painful to relate. If you love me, demand not what I wish to grant, but indeed cannot, without being a prey to the most torturing agony. Abuse not thy power over thy Henrietta. Adieu!

LETTER II.

NO longer will I deny your entreaties; your friendship deserves a sacrifice: I will make it in your favour, dear Susannah; I will forget myself. You shall know every anecdote of my life; the history of every thought, and of every feeling. I will hide nothing from you. Self-love I shall not listen to; truth will guide my pen. Adieu.

LETTER III.

HAPPILY blest with a sensible mother, the dawn of my infancy announced accomplishments which since have obtained your applauses, and the praises of men. Under the care of Mrs. Verman, the susceptibility of my mind, like marble under the chissel of Phidias, received the most exquisite form which taste and judgment can give. At sixteen, very few were the talents I did not possess; very few the sciences in which I was not an adept. The knowledge of the human heart Shakespeare displayed

displayed to me: his works, and the Spectator, taught me to think and to compare. The power of the passions I learned in ancient and modern history; their effects filled my soul with apprehension and diffidence; but when Nature began to bring forth their dormant seed in my heart, I trembled and shuddered at their opposition to the religious law. However strong the impression we imbibe in the earliest time of life, and sincere our resolution is never to alter them, the passions will talk, and silence reason. This truth I have experienced. Though prepared, and in arms against the seductions of pride and ambition, I have been subdued, and their slave. Would I had been born in a lonely cottage, far from men, and free from knowledge! I trusted to Reason for the conquest of pleasure; fool that I was not to know she spoke and acted like a coward, seemingly ready to engage, though determined to fly!

LETTER IV.

WHEN, from the involuntary pantings of my bosom, Mrs. Verman discovered that my heart began to beat to desire, she renewed her satire on man. I listened; but still my heart beat, and the monster man gave the impulse.

Like the child who, attracted by the beauty of a rose, advances eagerly his hand to pluck it up, and forgets the thorn which lies under it, we welcome the flattering temptation, totally neglectful of the evils it may bring upon us. Our senses put reason to defiance; we only think when pain or sorrow warns us of our imprudence.

The frightful picture my mother drew of man, however true in respect to his political life, my heart thought false in his character of a lover. This character nature formed with ingenuity: it is as inconsistent with falsehood as the wit of Lady Waldegrave with impertinence and foppery. Education changes not the real feelings of the human heart. Sentiments vary not as opinions.

Mr. Verman opposed her experience to my judgment. 'You expect,' said she to me one day, 'to be loved for

' yourself; that the man who will tell
' you of his passion will not feign it.
' This error has caused the ruin of
' many virtuous, unsuspecting maids;
' it leaves them defenceless against the
' attacks of their ungenerous enemy.'
And then she acquainted me with the character of a S——h, a R——y, and of a hundred more, who, under the mask of love and friendship, talked innocence into credulity, only to abuse, and then to abandon her to infamy and despair.

Such a corruption in the manners of men in the highest life, I would hardly believe. What was I to think of the rest of mankind, when those born to be an example of honour and virtue were living devotees to vice and perjury? Where are we to look for truth and integrity? These instances of open profligacy made me fearful: for a long time I hated the sight of men, and sought but in myself for happiness.

At eighteen, spite of sighs, oglings, whisperings, and publick homage of a crowd of adorers, my heart was my own; it was not to continue any longer passive under the load of indifference. The hour came when I yielded to the enchanting passion; when both love and nature, springing up a new life in me, their charms silenced my fears, and painted man as a friend.

LETTER V.

MRS. Verman and I were on a visit at an alderman's in the city, when a young gentleman of the most agreeable countenance entered the room with the familiar steps of friendship. Lady Bennet, the mistress of the house, presented him to us as a near relation lately come from Germany. A salute was given; but not received without a half blush, the natural effect of the concern forced by him in my breast. Never before had I seen fine features and modesty so happily blended: he looked as if insensible of his personal advantages; and talked not to be admired, but to please.

Lady Bennet appeared so sensibly proud of having such a nephew, that, my attention increasing in proportion to her esteem of him, I thought him the most accomplished young man I had

had ever beheld. 'It is not possible,' said I to myself, 'that a base soul can be lodged in so perfect a body! No! his heart must partake of the excellency of his person! Happy will be the woman he shall love!' After this private soliloquy, whose sense I took care not to trust to my eye, lest it's discovery should weaken the few charms I possessed, I played the woman, and acted the very reverse of what I thought.

I know, Susannah, that too easy a conquest is disdained; and that, oftener than our beauty, the glory of warming an insensible heart enflames a man to the enthusiasm of love. All passions are fed only by difficulties. A good under your hand palls presently, your desires. Life would be a torment, could we enjoy as soon as we wish.

The civilities of Mr. Romney (such was the gentleman's name) were not, for an hour, fixed to any particular object: he divided his attention between two young ladies and me; and neither of us had to boast his partiality. My pride called his behaviour injustice, and made me resolve on revenge. A city fop, the most unaccountable and ridiculous animal upon earth, mimicking the airs of a courtier, had impertinently leaned upon the back of my chair, and whispered a praise on my person; nay, swore he would bett ten to one in favour of my charms against all the women in England. This man, whom I had not deigned to answer, continuing to pester me with his assiduity, I dissembled my dislike, and dropped a few words which fixed him by me. His dear self importance was so pleased with the distinction I paid him, that, in the height of his gratitude, he displayed all his borrowed wit, and did not think it lost upon me.

A fool will sometimes be diverting, Susannah: the impertinencies of the fellow uttered had a novelty which amused me; like the tittle-tattle of children, they were so extravagantly mixed with a few sallies of good sense, that my wonder at that curious piece of folly gave me precisely the looks I wanted to humble Mr. Romney.

A man, however modest, is not dead to the desire of being esteemed; he necessarily knows his superiority when in opposition to a fop. My behaviour Mr. Romney felt. The error of my judgment he laid to the account of my heart: he thought me the more prepossessed, as I was the less rational. This idea deadened his vivacity; he answered a No for a Yes; and some traces of sadness were visible on his face. A side-glance I darted at him told me his uneasiness; and my heart panted with joy at the discovery. Fearful lest pride only should have worked Mr. Romney into a reverie and absence of mind, I artfully supported the fop's imagination with smiles of content. He had a fine voice: this he hinted to me; and, indeed, he exceeded my expectations. 'You should always sing, and not talk!' This I half whispered to him: the man took it for a compliment, bowed, and thanked me.

Women, Susannah, are better hypocrites than the most refined courtiers. Ambition may be easily seen through, their boasted love of independence; but passions lie buried in our hearts, as silent as the dead in their graves. Under the cloak of a natural levity, I concealed from every eye the inclination I began to feel; while Mr. Romney's impatient ingenuity to be his soul in every motion. There I read, I was the woman he loved! This intelligence changed not my plan: prudence told me to be false; and I continued the deceit.

LETTER VI.

A General silence, and a few yawnings, having succeeded to the eulogiums bestowed on Mr. Lewis's voice, cards were proposed, as the sole means not to feel the weight of time, the mortal enemy of the idle and stupid. Then Mr. Romney drew near me, opened his lips, and, with a sigh, closed them again. Unwilling to hear what I already knew, lest my sensibility should betray me, I arose, curtsied, and went to the whist-table.

In vain did Mr. Romney endeavour to trust my ear with the tale of his woe; in vain did he express in his eyes the secret of his heart: I feigned neither to hear, nor to see. My gaiety contrasted his languishing looks; and, though extremely delighted, he could not dissemble his passion: not once did he catch in my features the satisfaction I enjoyed.

'So

'So handsome; yet so indifferent!'

I turned my head, frowned, and carelessly attended to my game.

'Indifferent! I was wrong!—Mr. Lewis is the man!'

'Trump!' exclaimed I; and I played the ace of diamonds. Mr. Romney returned to the chimney-corner; but not, however, before he had complimented me with—' I have seen you! I am undone!'

Give a child the toy he longs for, he will throw it aside, and wish for another; deny it to him, you will enhance it's value, and endear it to his fancy. Thus man must be treated, or disgust will follow his enjoyment.

My fop, and my discretion, helped me the whole evening against the attacks of my already enamoured heart. It's emotions—guests I never had entertained before—I treated with the familiarity of habit; and not once Mr. Romney, though watching attentively every smile, and every word, could suspect his power over me.

Dissimulation I discarded when I came home.

'How do you like Lady Bennet's nephew, Henrietta?' asked Mrs. Verman.

That question I answered with sincerity. My mother had too much experience not to discover a lover in my praises of Mr. Romney.

'I own,' said she, with a sneer, 'that he may, at a first sight, prejudice in his favour. Were the virtues of a man centered in an exquisitely-made shape and comely presence, he would certainly deserve the eulogiums you have lavished upon him; but, Miss, these are too often the deluding qualities under which are concealed vice and folly. Study the character before you judge of the man: not to your heart, but to your reason, apply for the knowledge of mankind. The old woman whom you mistook once at the opera for a beauty, so much altered by patches and paint her features were, is the picture of all the objects before you. The senses are not the judges of truth.'

And then, fixing her eyes upon mine—

'As Mr. Romney is but an acquaintance, your good opinion of him is an harmless error. It matters not what you think of people in his situation of life, since it is not amongst them you are to look for a friend, or a husband. My Henrietta is worthy of a nobler fate.'

The sense of this speech told so expressly that she would not favour my new inclination, that I immediately declared her views for my establishment were the more agreeable; that they perfectly coincided with my ambition, and would contribute to her happiness. So easy and natural was the tone of my voice, that the suspicious Mrs. Verman doubted not my veracity: she embraced me; and, a few minutes after, I retired to my apartment.

LETTER VII.

I Was no sooner alone than I reflected on the inconsistency of our passions. My mother loved me with the utmost tenderness, yet could not think to see me happy but in her own way: to her feelings I was to chain my sensibility; and, at the impetuous season of desires, adopt the cool reason of a woman of forty. A nobleman for her son-in-law was the real cause of her unceasing fondness. What fondness is that which my opposition to her choice would have easily changed into hatred? It was too evident she loved me but for herself. This thought made me not forget the benefits I had received from her: I remembered, with gratitude, the peculiar care she had taken of my education. To her I was indebted for every quality I had to boast: but was I, in her hands, like a curious piece of mechanism in those of an ingenious artist, to be made use of only for her personal advantage? Both my heart and reason exclaimed a 'No!' I could not think to be led forcibly to the arms of an undeserving husband, like the unfortunate victims of the French pride, who, to the everlasting disgrace of humanity, are buried for life in the walls of a convent. The laws of England are the friends of Nature: we detest the inhuman sacrifices she is perpetually compelled to make in the countries governed by ignorance, despotism, and superstition!

I resolved, Susannah, on attempting to erase from my heart the memory of Mr.

Mr. Romney; (it was all filial duty could require from me) and on loving, if the attempt proved unsuccessful. This determination calmed my mind, and lulled me to rest.

LETTER VIII.

MY first thought, when I awoke, was about Mr. Romney; and almost half an hour was devoted to him: I could not help it. The next reverie was on the means to reconcile my mother's peace with my own; and this, to my sorrow, could not be effected without hypocrisy. I had too much virtue to be true at the expence of her happiness: besides, I flattered myself that the present advantages resulting from a marriage with a man of Mr. Romney's fortune, would overbalance the brilliant uncertainty she fed her imagination with. From a woman, with whose ambitious disposition I was perfectly acquainted, it was not wise to expect such a sacrifice: but she was my mother; I hated to think her imprudent and ungenerous.

* * *

Mrs. Verman took me into her closet after breakfast. The air of mystery she had assumed when she bid me follow her, and the orders she gave not to be interrupted, announcing plainly the subject of her conversation, I put myself on my guard, and defied her sagacity.

'Sit down, Henrietta; and listen, not to a mother, but a friend, who knows the world, and will not deceive you.

'You are at an age when the passions, commanding an absolute obedience to their dictates, throw the head into confusion, and blind our understanding. Once the slaves of desire, it is not in our power to remove the veil spread between reason and us. To free you from the danger of such a situation is my duty.

'The ingenuity of youth is an enemy to their happiness: like honour in the man who wants to be preferred, it is a weapon we furnish a villain with against ourselves; a weapon the more secure in his hand, as our hearts are incessantly exposed to the blow it strikes.

'Consider mankind under the two classes of knaves and fools. However shocking this assertion may be to your good-nature, believe it true. The principles of education are never so deeply rooted, but they sooner or later give way to the maxims of the society we live in. Had you, with the eye of a philosopher, observed the actions of the persons you have visited, heard, and conversed with, you would have easily distinguished between their tongues and hearts, their countenances and judgment. Every sensible man or woman adopts indifferently the character of those they want to please or deceive. As virtue, like the language of a pedantick fellow, is entirely out of fashion with the polite world, and this polite world contains the very choice of a nation, we readily assent to their opinions, rather than to be laughed at, and ranked among the vulgar. Thus pride forms our second education the more prevailing over the former, that it agrees with our desires, and favours every passion.

'The whole end of this life, Henrietta, is to pass it away in as much pleasure and as little pains as we can. Fortune, and a high rank, procure us every bliss, when we know how to enjoy them: they are the miraculous spring which washes every fault, and turns foibles into perfections.

'Trust to sentiment for happiness, no more than you would take a blind man for your guide in a thorny path bordered with precipices. Love is a word with which we ennoble the wants of the senses. Did we examine our hearts, and conclude impartially from their longings, we should own, that man in general, and not this or that, is the object of our wishes. It may happen, that a similarity of disposition will cause what they call sympathy, and fix our affections upon one in preference to another: but those who are well acquainted with humanity, will convince you, Henrietta, that a perfect harmony, like a total difference between two characters, is incompatible with real happiness. Dislike or hatred must be our lot, when we can command bliss, or cannot entertain the hope of ever enjoying it.

'Constancy

'Constancy is a forced state, which, like a delirium, supposes the patient incapable of reflecting: it cannot subsist long, unless the passions be kept in a perpetual ferment; and experience tells us that none outlive the possession of the objects we pant after. This the lovers will not suffer reason to demonstrate, till indifference has taught them their error.

'Folly, Henrietta, is not peculiar to love; it belongs to every other passion of the heart and mind: it is a general disease, more or less dangerous, according as we are more or less infected with it.'

LETTER IX.

'THERE is a foible in our character, which owes it's birth to the establishment of society, and is more powerful and lasting than any of the passions we are fated to feel: that foible is pride; it begins at the prime of life, and vanishes only upon the death-bed; nay, often survives the horrors which then surround us, and reigns in the will it dictates. As a Christian, I detest it's sway: as a woman, I yield to it. Religion and philosophy avail not against the pleasure of living in all the luxuriancy of greatness and independence. The superiority of our charms over those of our rivals procures not half the delight we enjoy in the respects and compliance of a world of courtiers. Elegant equipages, sumptuous tables, costly dresses, and a splendid retinue, leave not our souls the time of thinking: every sense is constantly gratified and kept alive by variety, and the brilliant imagination of the numberless slaves, whose only study is to divert and to please.

'Pride, instead of decaying, like love, is daily increasing in our hearts: it knows not the transitions from raptures to disgust, but is always new and enchanting; it has in our old age the same charms it possessed in our youth. Never an abatement is sensible in the transports it causes.

'The wise, Henrietta, believe not in the reality of love; but all agree that pride exists naturally: they compare the man we prefer to a silk we chuse amongst a thousand at Van Sommers; rather as the effect of the necessity of making a choice than of the resolves of our taste and judgment. That man and that silk have the same fate: it is needless to tell you the consequence.

'Your beauty and accomplishments call daily the homages of men in the highest life: by them only are you esteemed at your real value. Like an excellent picture from the Roman school, which is unnoticed by the ignorant, and admired by the virtuoso, you are praised by the great, the sole connoisseurs in wit, talents, and sensibility. Your perfections, among a lower class of mankind, would be entirely lost; and, perhaps, thought as many defects. I have once seen a savage shutting his ears to the most perfect harmony; and heard him say he could not conceive what pleasure such a confusion could afford. How many men are like that savage!

'Exert your reason, that you may not be a dupe to your heart: look on all men with indifference, and leave to pride the disposal of your hand. This foible once satisfied, life is a continual scene of bliss.'

LETTER X.

THE manner of delivery, and the art of the speaker, convince oftener than the reasons with which he defends his opinion. Our vanity, alarmed at the superiority he may gain, is ever ready to oppose the latter; but our hearts are easily subdued by the former. Truth and falshood are equally credited when the orator talks to our passions, and not to our understanding.

Mr. Romney had not made such an impression upon me as to make me insensible of the real advantages inherent in titles and grandeur: these I had been long accustomed to consider as the rights of beauty; and my imagination, more than once, had enjoyed all their charms. The panegyrick Mrs. Verman made of them awakened my ambition, and forced a smile from my lips.

My mother, attentive to my motions, guessed the approbation my heart gave.

'I am

'I am glad, Henrietta, that it is in your power to determine for yourself. The woman who listens to the insidious language of passion, like the religious enthusiast, is a satire on human reason. Continue to be cool, and not mistake illusion for reality: one error is the spring of thousands. From the emotions your soul is affected with, form not your judgment of them: there are hours when we are absolutely unable to compare and to judge. The passions inebriate the soul: at that time, like those of the man intoxicated with liquor, her faculties are in a total inertness, or in a deadly agony.

'Trust to me your feelings, Henrietta, when their novelty will strike you; I will then tell you their nature, and administer their antidote. A distemper, though ever so bad, is easily removed, when, at it's first appearance, a skilful physician is called; but, if we leave the cure to time, or our own abilities, it makes such a progress as to defy art and experience.'

LETTER XI.

MY inclination for Mr. Romney, Susannah, engaged not upon equal terms with my self-love: as readily did I at last acknowledge the authority of Mrs. Verman's counsels, as if he had been an absolute stranger to me. No resistance of any moment was made: although the first onset had announced victory, it was not supported; and my mother's triumph was compleat. I blushed at the surprize of my senses, and told her the power of their illusions over my judgment.

'I wonder not, Henrietta, at your having been moved by the presence of an handsome man. Beauty, in both sexes, has irresistible charms; the sensations it gives are as pleasing as natural: but it is like a rose we smell, like a melodious voice we hear; whilst we breathe the perfume, or listen, we forget the thorn, and want of taste.

'I do not intend to make the satire of Mr. Romney: he may possess as noble a soul as his shape is excellent, he endowed with every virtue, and deserving of your love and esteem; but he may also be the reverse of what I suppose him to be. Were I to judge of him from the education he has received, and the unexpected turn of fortune which made his father rich, and enables him to gratify every call of his passions, I might, without injuring his character, be prejudiced against him: he looks grave and sedate, it is true; but no mien whatever is a proof of our wisdom and morality. The real inclinations of men and women I do not search for in their air, since fashion and want have made us a necessity of being false. You will tell me that Mr. Romney, not having been brought up within the atmosphere of St. James's, has not perhaps adopted the polite vices of a courtier. It is an error, Henrietta: these vices are not the property of the great; their refinements, I own, nobody has but themselves. None, with such a good grace, will tell a lie; will caress a man into the belief of their friendship whilst they solicit his disgrace; and pant for pleasures they cannot enjoy without violating the laws, or driving a whole family to despair. These advantages are the effects of a long habit, and the noble assurance peculiar to high birth and power*. If you except the heroism of being openly a deist, a libertine, and an adulterer, you will find that almost every individual in the society is tainted with the same vices and follies. Fear hides the corrupted heart of a commoner; to that only you may ascribe the appearance of more virtue in the citizen than in the man of the world. Since, then, Henrietta, you cannot flatter yourself to know the man of true honour amongst a thousand hypocrites, would you hesitate in the choice of an husband? With the great you will be censured, but respected: the spleen of the plebeian, raised by their superiority over him, never goes so far as to annihilate

---

* Like me, the reader must take this for a satire rather than for Mrs. Verman's real opinion: though seemingly in earnest, she had too much sense not to know the errors she commended. Had she painted them to her daughter under their true colours, she would not have acted the part she wanted to perform.

'his servility; he murmurs, shakes his chain, but continues the slave. A false step in a woman of the city exposes her to contempt and misery; in a lady it is called gallantry, and announces to the publick her beauty and merit. For one husband, unfashionable enough to take the alarm, and sue for a divorce, hundreds laugh at a disgrace they could not avoid, or seem not to know it. An amiable companion, rather than a faithful wife, is the taste of the great. Sensible that sentiment has it's ebb and flow, they do not require a constancy which their reason proves to them to be a chimera, the hobby-horse of the fools and humble tradesmen. Such an enlightened indifference you cannot expect from the latter: their base-born souls are entirely taken up with the ideas of order and decency; which, among the polite, are but as many incentives to enjoy.

'Your virtue, Henrietta, needs not this picture to determine your choice in favour of men of quality: I am conscious you detest the thought of ever abusing the man you will bless with your hand; but what in one hour appears impossible to happen, may in the next, by the power of circumstances, come to pass. Did a young man, of a generous disposition, think he would rob, at fifty, his countrymen of several millions? No: it is Fortune's fault: the temptations she laid before him were too strong for his virtue; he could not possibly resist, and therefore turned a plunderer and a villain.

'No man, no woman, premeditates a crime in cool blood: so long as we reason we abhor it; but when passion takes the sway, it loses all it's horrors; and ten to one we commit it. Like the talents of a general, which are not generally esteemed before he meets and defeats an enemy as brave as himself, our virtues are absolutely unknown till we have opposed the seductions of desire, and conquered.'

LETTER XII.

THE maxims of Mrs. Verman, though most of them the contrast of her conduct and of my way of thinking, pleased my mind, and obliterated the charms of Mr. Romney. So cool were her contempt of the citizen, and her esteem of the great, that my theory in the knowledge of mankind yielded readily to the authority of her practical experience. How could I mistrust her assertions, when the life she had led among the different classes of men had needs taught her their real worth? Books tell not the passions of men so well as a constant intercourse with them: a few days of familiar conversation betray a heart which the history of it's feelings does not always unfold. Too often does an author mistake his own affections for those of the personages he gives a part to perform in the novel he writes; too often is he a slave to prejudice, and draws a false picture. For one Montesquieu who composes for the men of all nations, how many only for the society they live in! The same partiality which guides the pen of political writers, you easily discover in those of the memoirs which are daily published: to them both might be justly applied the following French line for a device—

Ii rs nous et nos amis, nul n'aura de Mérite.

My mother's conversation restored the calm to my heart. If I thought of Mr. Romney, it was only with the half pleasure we feel at the second sight of a fine perspective, or the repetition of a bon-mot. Lest, however, his presence should revive the past illusion, and wheedle me out of the hopes of a grandeur I flattered myself to enjoy one day, I resolved on not seeing him. A tender woman should never suffer the visits of the man she fears, when her reason is weak enough to dissemble the reality of the danger she runs. Nature is not an enemy to be easily conquered: she laughs at our boasted prudence, and often defeats it at the very minute we are the more certain of our triumph. I trusted not to reason for victory; but desired my mother to prevent, by her care, the return of a sentiment, which, as I had once indulged it, might again be welcome to my heart.

LETTER XIII.

MY confidence in Mrs. Verman endeared me to her; she no longer saw in me the child she had born,
but

but the woman she had educated. Like a lump of clay, which the art of the sculptor metamorphoses into a Venus, from her I had received a form which shewed the merit of the artist. I was a work her reason only had to boast: her empire over my mind flattered her the more, that she affected to have none over my person.

'I abjure the power which nature 'and the laws have given me over you.' Had she told me when the solidity of my judgment answered for my discretion—' I will direct your choice, but 'never force mine upon you.'

Thus, Susannah, by seemingly leaving me to myself, she had artfully disposed my heart to feel agreeably to her dictates, and not to perceive that I acted as she pleased. The art of an orator is to arm the passions one against another, and appear rather to adopt the opinion of his auditors than to establish his own. Whoever knows how to flatter our pride, is the master of our affection: at his voice, vice and virtue, wisdom and folly, change their nature, and obtain alternately our esteem or contempt.

* *

SOME days passed without my hearing from Mr. Romney. I will own to you, that I was not a little piqued at the indifference of a man whom I had thought deeply enamoured of me. My pride hated to reflect on the mistake I had made; and, far from welcoming this new remedy against him, I was heartily vexed he himself had furnished me with it. However determined not to love, I could not help wishing for his tenderness: his insensibility was a disgrace to my charms. When their power is in question, Susannah, what woman will not resent the affront, and meditate a revenge?

'I will lay all the illusions of beauty 'in ambush for him; and when his 'heart has surrendered, treat it with 'all the haughtiness of an offended 'conqueror: from me he shall have no 'mercy; he shall suffer all the tortures 'of an unhappy passion.'

These counsels of my indignation I concealed from Mrs. Verman, lest she should point to me the danger attached to the attempt, and dissuade me from it. More than one indiscreet vain maid has lost her liberty, and been chained with the fetters she destined to the rebel of insensible. That truth glanced on my mind; there nothing could penetrate and fix, but the means of gratifying my pride and assuring my success.

LETTER XIV.

MRS. Verman and I were walking in Richmond Park, when, at the turning of an avenue we met with Lady Bennet. The first cast of my eyes was in favour of her nephew: I looked for him, and saw him not. We had not been long with Lady Bennet, before she whispered me—

'How chagrined Mr. Romney will 'be, not to have attended me to Richmond, when he hears you was there! 'I am certain that the pleasures he has 'been desired to partake at Hampstead 'will not compensate for the loss of 'your company.'

'At his age, Madam, that loss is 'insensible. Young men, in the midst 'of their amusements, think not of 'another happiness. Very easily can 'he find a woman more agreeable and 'entertaining: the assurance of the 'contrary is only a compliment paid to 'vanity, mere fashionable words, on 'which reason sets no value.'

'Indeed, Miss, you wrong my nephew. His good sense scorns to tell 'what he does not think; never will 'he sacrifice truth to the honour of 'passing for a polite man. He told 'me of his love for you: I answer for 'his veracity.'

'Of his love for me? Ah! ah! ah! 'This jest I did not expect from you, 'my lady.'

'I am in earnest, Miss; and, if your 'heart has no objection, his hand is at 'your commands.'

'These words confirm the jest, Madam. What man of any prudence 'would so quickly determine for matrimony with a woman whose inclinations he is hardly acquainted with; 'venture the happiness of his whole 'life to gratify a caprice? The man 'who submits not his taste to the examination of his judgment is not a 'husband for me. Levity, in a business of so great a moment, shews not 'Mr. Romney to his advantage. he is 'too prudent to consult but his fancy 'in the choice of his wife.'

'He is enchanted with your beauty;

'and I have convinced him of your virtues.'

'Talk no more; talk no more!'

And, with a smile, I put my hand on her lips, and joined Mrs. Verman.

LETTER XV.

SO easy a conquest, my lady, no longer flattered my vanity. My indignation subsided; and had Mr. Romney appeared then before us, I would have received him with the killing gaiety of indifference.

Lady Bennet attempted a second whisper: I turned my ear.

'Listen to me.'

And she took me by the hand.

'Well, what have you to say, dear Madam?'

'Think of my nephew. You cannot be insensible to his passion for you; can you?'

'Pray, Madam, spare me the repetition of that nonsense. I am free, absolutely free; and leave the disposal of my hand to my mother.'

'To you only will he be indebted for it; your mother's consent is but an acceffary to his happiness. What would her consent avail a man of delicacy, were yours to be influenced by it? Freely return love for love. My nephew is charming; he has wit, riches, and generofity. With him, every wifh you may form shall be satisfied; he will breathe but to please, and make you supremely happy. He has seen you but once; but can you from hence question his sincerity? Reflect on yourself, and consult not your modefty. Are not you conscious he muft love?'

What a dangerous flatterer this Lady Bennet! Such an art in a knight's wife! I know not what reply I would have made, had not Mrs. Verman called for me. I instantly tripped to her; and the glow which Lady Bennet had raised on my cheek retreated into my heart.

No more did I leave my mother, and lend my ears to the too eloquent, persuasive tongue, of Lady Bennet. One minute, however, she found, as we left the park, to press my hand, and enforce her action with the following words.

'The more I know you, the more I wifh you for my niece. My poor nephew! how he loves you! Would you believe it, your heart would melt with sympathy, and—'

I curtsied, and stepped into the coach.

LETTER XVI.

THE certainty of my triumph destroyed all the merit of Mr. Romney. I compared him to a beautiful decoration, which pleases the eye, and affects not the foul; though, till it vanishes, every fenfe feems to enjoy. When this mistake in our fenfations warms a head in favour of an object, the heart catches neceffarily the diftemper, and feels pleafurably under the delufions of a prepoffeffed fancy. A doctor, infatuated with an error, defends it with all the fire and eloquence of a devotee to truth. We all are that doctor. Who among mankind can fay he knows himfelf, and acts according to reafon?

'I love not,' said I to my mother, when we fat in the coach; 'I love not. Had not Lady Bennet convinced me of her nephew's attachment to me, I might have endangered my liberty from too eager a defire of captivating him. He is mine; no longer am I his.'

And then I related to her the project I had formed.

'True woman!' exclaimed she, tapping her fan upon my shoulder; 'true woman! We never make ufe of our underftanding but when in no need of it.'

To compleat my cure, Mrs. Verman propofed to flip the remainder of the evening at Lady B——y's rout.

'There, Henrietta, in the amazement which the diverfity of many hundred characters will caufe, you will lofe the idea of Mr. Romney. Be not offended at the publick, private, or familiar homage which men will pay to your charms, and at the loud whifperings which envy or ill-nature will force from the women againft you. Have no ears in the polite world; and move your eyes but to applaud.

'The art of ufing our organs is of the greateft importance; and it should be the principal part of our education;
'but

'but the ignorant low wretches en-
'trusted with it, like a painter's boy,
'whose sole study is to prepare the co-
'lours, leave to genius and experience
'the finishing of our minds. A man
'of fortune lavishes thousands of
'pounds a year upon horses and fur-
'niture; and grudges a few hundreds
'for perfecting the reason of his chil-
'dren! Instead of chusing a governor
'among the adepts in the science of the
'world, he picks up a base-born fel-
'low, whose whole understanding is
'confined to the opinions of the uni-
'versity he has lived in. This is the
'spring of most of the imprudences
'young men are guilty of at their first
'appearance in society. Like an ex-
'tensive thick-set, unfrequented forest,
'which offers no retreat to the bewil-
'dered traveller against the attacks
'of wild beasts, the stage of the un-
'known social life has no asylum for
'an innocent heart against falshood
'and perfidy. Youth, taught only
'what they ought not to believe or
'practise, must needs be a prey to er-
'rors, vice, and folly.

'The education of women, Hen-
'rietta, is still more unenlightened.
'The modern plans are the full mea-
'sure of stupidity, the fittest I ever
'knew or heard of to turn a head, and
'corrupt a heart. A virgin at fifteen
'is no less a wonder to me than a dis-
'creet man at eighteen. The exist-
'ence of these two beings is as incon-
'sistent with the manner they are
'brought up, as ambition with an ab-
'solute want of talents.'

※ ※

WE were then within a few yards
of Lady B——y's house. An hundred
carriages announcing a numerous assembly; though elegantly dressed, and
of a form to be admired, I felt a fear,
and as instantly a colouring declared it
to Mrs. Verman.

'As Lady B——y's rout is the ren-
'dezvous of almost all the people of
'fashion, and it is the first time you
'venture among such a number of
'them, I owe you one advice.
'Blush not when you enter the apart-
'ments, but present yourself with the
'ease of a woman habituated to act in
'the brilliant scenes of life. Were
'they to perceive the smallest altera-
'tion in your features, diffidence in
'your steps, and confusion in the com-
'pliments you will pay or return, their
'pride would shew you immediately
'their superiority. The woman who
'differs in her dress, her speech, and
'her countenance, or mimicks only
'those of the company she visits, is con-
'sidered by them as an exotick trans-
'planted on a foreign soil; the shadow
'of a reality. Resume your spirits,
'Henrietta, and yield them not an ad-
'vantage you partake with them.
'Your modesty you should leave in
'the coach; it is a bad companion
'among the great; it may murder the
'inexpressible charms of your shape,
'and rob your graces of their enchant-
'ing play. Never forget that a becom-
'ing vice is much more esteemed than
'an aukward virtue.'

LETTER XVII.

LIKE a sensible Frenchman, who
never beheld but the borrowed
charms of the ladies of Paris, on entering Ranelagh fixes upon a beauty
wherever he casts his eyes, and at that
heavenly sight thinks himself in a ter-
restrial paradise, my soul panted with
delight at the first glance I threw before
and round me in Lady B——y's apartment. Though I had many times added to the number of the idle and the
gay at a lady of quality's rout, never
had I seen the same sumptuosity and
magnificence displayed. My admiration did not, however, confuse my head;
I curtsied, talked, listened, and answered,
with all the coolness of a satisfied pride.
The respect shewed me by some noblemen of our acquaintance, called soon
the general attention; men and women
with the most impertinent curiosity
eyed me from head to foot: from the
smiles of the former, and the uneasiness
of the latter, I quickly discovered I
made a tolerable figure. The spite of
our own sex is the best panegyrick of
our charms: words have not half it's
expression and eloquence, and it is the
more flattering, that it is forced from
our real enemies.

※ ※

So volatile a company, so dissipated,
and seemingly more devoted to pleasure
than to sentiment, made me fancy every
individual out of the reach of the passions. 'Whoever thinks not,' said I
to myself, 'cannot feel;' and really
their

their language and manners belied reason, wit, and common sense.

Mrs. Verman read in my heart.

'That behaviour and that language, Henrietta, which offend your sensibility, are the effects of a refined politick. Thoughtlessness is the excuse for the faults rank and fortune do not justify, and a guard against the indiscretions of too open a character; they save the trouble to blush, and defeat the hatred of an enemy, or the sagacity of a rival. Another time I will explain to you the hidden mysteries of such a conduct, and convince you of it's propriety. It is enough now to assure you, that none here are really what they appear to be.'

'But the old, Madam, why do they play the fools? The levity of youth agrees with the wrinkles on their faces no more than the libertinism of a bishop with the sanctity of his station. Their airs and their age are the most incompatible things I ever saw: their union is a most violent satire of reason and decency. I wish I had not beheld the odious spectacle.'

'When you know mankind better, you will take these contradictions as the natural effects of a social life. The fear of being forsaken when we can no longer procure a diversion or a pleasure, compels us to assume the looks of approbation and indulgence; by conforming, in appearance, to the follies of young people, we ennoble and authorize them; their gratitude gives, in return, respects and attendance. Thus our pride enjoys when every other sentiment is dead. The miseries of a solitude, after having long lived in the world, are not to be borne. We must still see, talk, and slander. A woman who has not that comfort at sixty might as well be buried; the torment of reflecting is worse than death; hardly one in ten thousand can think coldly on the past, and be a tolerable companion to herself.

'Continue your observations, Henrietta. This is a school where you may form your judgment, and then be in no need of a guide in the thorny path of life. I advise you not to shew so much wit, that they may think they have more than you: this superiority, rather than that of beauty, most women are desirous to possess, as the latter is the gift of nature, and the former their own work. Allow them that advantage, and your own rivals will praise you.'

LETTER XVIII.

SUCH a group of foolish heads, though the greatest part of them esteemed the wisest of the nation, plunged me a few minutes into a sad reverie, and caused the following soliloquy.

'What men! what women! This the chosen set of mankind recommended me by my mother! The circle into which she destines me to move! However plausible her justification of them, no real worth can be hid under so visible a contempt of themselves. He who has merit is fond of glory, and not of shame. She who has virtue, prides not in the airs of vice. Their folly is too natural to be affected. What! not one thought that can reveal their reason! Every where the looks of self-sufficiency! Have we, then, no other value than that we receive from a costly dress and a graceful mien! People so much taken up with their dear persons cannot concern themselves in another's happiness; their souls must be totally dead to tender feelings: love, pity, and generosity, are unknown to them; their affections centre in them, in them only. How can a woman resist long the pressing passions of her heart, and the attacks of a lover, when her virtue is not supported by the esteem and tenderness of her husband! How can this not hate his wife, when cards, dissipation, and the desire of pleasing, are the delights she prefers to his attachment? Oh! true happiness proceeds from our feelings, and not the vain satisfaction of a false pride! It may be a torment to be deprived at once of the appearances of rank and fortune; but when we enjoy them, poor, poor indeed, is the pleasure they give!'

Then, Susannah, I thought of Mr. Romney; take my word for it. From my comparing him to the company I was with, he gained infinitely in my esteem. I reflected on a conjugal life, unlivened enlivened by a mutual love: it appeared to me the only bliss to be wished for. I sighed at the ambition of my mother.

LETTER XIX.

THE men were too politely bred up not to offend my modesty with the tender of their homage. My charms, for an hour, were the topick of their indefatigable tongues. Never before were my ears stunned with such a torrent of impertinent eulogiums. I was an angel just escaped from Heaven for the delight of mankind, the only temptation the devil could reasonably think of to plunge them deeper and deeper into sin. No woman could be without envy, no man without love, at the sight of so transcendent a beauty: what quarrels, what dissentions, I would cause in society!

Thus, dear Susannah, was I pestered and tormented, till a fine lady stopped this tide of falshood and civility, by desiring me to make one with her at quadrille.

'I never play, Madam.'

This answer confounded her.

'You never play! Amazing!'

And, shrugging her shoulders up with contempt, left me, with—'Good God! what company has she kept!'

'Pray, Miss,' asked another, with the supercilious air of a new-made countess, 'since you do not play, how do you kill the tedious hours of an evening? For my part, I would die were I to tell them by myself at my chimney-corner. How do you murder them away, Miss?'

'In the conversation, my lady, of a few of my mother's chosen friends.'

'But, Miss, we cannot always chatter.'

'We think, Madam.'

'You think! Ah! ah! ah! that is odd enough! Fine diversion indeed!'

And, with the smile of pity, she went to whisper my answer to every card-table.

The singularity of my replies freed me from my admirers; they could not, with honour to themselves, differ in my favour from the opinion of a quality-toast. I was truly a very fine creature; but how could I have any merit, since I played not at cards, and durst to boast I thought sometimes? This judgment formed upon me, I read in almost every look: some smiled their approbation of me; but none presumed to take my part.

LETTER XX.

MY mother was upon the rack; I saw it: but honest pride had prevailed over false vanity; I was insensible of her sufferings.

'A pretty world this!' said I to myself: 'they courted me when they took me for a fool, and forsake me when I prove I am not so!'

The reflected contempt they inspired me for them, spread itself on my countenance; nor did I attempt to conceal it. Ready wit, or superiority of birth, had not availed me so much: it gave me an importance which struck these little souls, and gave again a life to their deceitful flattering tongue. Had I betrayed a sensibility at the affront intended upon me, I should have been avoided and laughed at: but my indifference announcing both my knowledge of the world, and my disdain of them, their haughtiness vanished, and I was once more courted and admired.

This sudden turn threw the countess into no small confusion. From the bad opinion she entertained for the company, she had hoped they would not perceive the advantage she had given me, or side with me against an heroick supporter of their invaded rights. Like an army of scribblers, always ready to engage the first genius who dares to monopolize the publick esteem, the fools of quality should constantly stand in defence of one another, and with sneers, jargon, and scorn, beat their enemy out of the field.

For the first time, the sense of her folly brought a glow on the cheeks of a fine lady; spite of her fan, which she placed between her shame and us, I discovered it. It was not the colouring of an humbled pride, but of the consciousness of having acted contrary to the dictates of her heart. This discovery made me her friend, at the same time that it filled me with indignation against the manners of the age, which had thus ennobled falshood and impertinence, to the disgrace of nature and reason.

My

My mistake of the countess's character made me instantly repeal the sentence I had pronounced against the men and women before me. They might all, for what I knew, wear the same mask, and have a soul the very contrast of their air. Does the moral he preaches tell always the real sentiments of a clergyman; and a promise, on his honour, the integrity of a nobleman? No; not one in twenty agrees with his sermons, or his words: their hearts are in a perpetual contradiction with their tongues. How difficult to know mankind! That knowledge we can acquire no more than that of ourselves: like the mysteries, they bid defiance to our reason and experience.

LETTER XXI.

I Must not for the future believe the appearances; but, like a circumspect philosopher, wait till every doubt be elucidated to form my judgment.

This resolution reconciled me to the company; whom I looked then upon as a particular kind of men who had their own language, opinions, and manners; and whose hearts, doubly guarded by pride and policy, never trusted their real feelings to the indiscretion of a look or a feature. I went so far in their favour, as to doubt whether their apparent folly was not true wisdom, since the generality of mankind continued to prostrate at their feet, adore their whims, and be ruled by them.

These changes in my way of thinking were the natural effects of the different lights under which they appeared to me. I was in the case of a man who, seeing a cameleon in a green colour, thought it was it's genuine form, till he perceived it turned into white, then black, then red, according to the various-coloured objects near which it stood. The diversity of the characters of those whom he has interest to please or deceive, is the coloured object from which the great borrow their countenances; and so expressive is then the figure they put on, that within a few hours they may rationally be esteemed or despised.

Tired to listen, and be compelled to smother every blush their perpetual attacks on my delicacy called on my cheeks, I got up; and, after having walked round several card-tables, stepped to that where the countess played. So much of good-nature and friendship was in my looks, that she beheld me without hatred. This passion, as a specifick against the sense of our injustice, prevails so often in the hearts of those who offend, that the absence of it in the countess confirmed my esteem of her.

There was by her an empty chair. She looked at it; then smiled upon me. I understood her, and sat down. She stooped to my ear.

'I was a fool—forgive. Upon the 'stage my rank has placed me, there 'are parts I am obliged to perform, to 'comply with the taste of the specta-'tor. The more we swerve from na-'ture, and depart from other men's 'opinions and manner of acting, the 'greater our glory, the louder and 'more incessant the applauses they be-'stow. Though sensible that our tri-'umphs are the contempt of the wise, 'these are so few, compared to the 'multitude who admire us, that our 'reason argues always in favour of 'our pride: add to this the silly at-'tempts of the publick, which afford 'us as much pleasure as Holland's 'servile imitation of Garrick's man-'ner gives a disgust to the best judges 'of theatrical merit; and you will 'cease to wonder we still continue to 'wear a mask which every body endea-'vours to take away from us, to adorn 'themselves with. Let us be friends, 'Miss; you will find me worthy of 'your esteem: to you I will shew the 'woman I must conceal from the pub-'lick eye. Merit, in the polite world, 'has the fate of an ill-written novel, 'it is an intruder, whose sight is con-'stantly detested and avoided.'

Her partner then begging she would attend to her cards—

'If you despise me not, Miss, come 'to see me; I will be proud of an inti-'macy with you. Will you?'

I curtsied to her invitation, and promised to go.

LETTER XXII.

'WHAT!' said I to myself, as I was going to Mrs. Verman; 'for the sake only of differing 'from

'from their inferiors, the great degrade
' themselves from the dignity of man,
' and leave, shamelessly, to those they
' scorn, the appearances of a superiority
' of merit and virtue! Is it possible
' that the ingenuity and good-sense of
' the Countess Mortimer should be
' such a defect as to expose her to a
' blush, or the secret malicious whis-
' pers of a polite circle, were she bold
' enough to talk and behave in cha-
' racter! A torment to a generous
' heart must be a life thus forcibly de-
' voted to falshood and folly. They
' look happy; it is a lye. Happiness
' cannot consist in the perpetual sa-
' crifice of our tastes and inclinations,
' in the frivolous regard of those we
' despise, or in the natural contempt
' we must have of ourselves. The
' pleasures of pride are not a compen-
' sation for the loss of the publick es-
' teem; their indifference of it is not
' sincere: every man, every woman,
' unless absolutely insensible of ho-
' nour, is proud to obtain and deserve
' it.'

Far from healing the wound which my heart had received, the company renewed it's sensibility. The despair of ever enjoying happiness with a courtier, who, from his circumstances in life, had none to procure, revived the idea of Mr. Romney. ' A man of his
' rank had not the noble privilege of
' being a fool, without incurring the
' contempt of the world: on his me-
' rit only could he rely for an honour-
' able distinction in a society, where
' fortune, unattended by a high birth,
' entitles not the individuals to the
' airs, vices, and follies of people of
' quality. When the depravity of our
' hearts is not encouraged by flatterers
' and the insignificancy of our enemies,
' we seldom laugh voluntarily at mo-
' rality, and give a loose to every de-
' sire. From Mr. Romney's real ne-
' cessity of obeying the calls of ho-
' nour and decency, I may safely con-
' clude he is the man my reason must
' prefer.'

Certain that the knowledge of this last thought would displease Mrs. Verman, I took care to conceal it from her.

' So thoughtful, Henrietta, in this
' gay circle?'

' I am not well, Madam; I am as
' much suffocated from the want of air,
' as tired with their senseless praises.
' Modesty is here in a perpetual ago-
' ny: it seems they out-vie one ano-
' ther in their attacks against her; and
' exert all the powers of refined civi-
' lity to give her the deadly blow.
' Though you have taught me to an-
' swer their language, you have not
' made me insensible of the poison it
' contains. In vain does the ambi-
' tious gild the pill of infamy to con-
' quer the scruples of the man he wants;
' this soon parts it from it's talisman,
' and sees it as it is. My feigned in-
' difference is an injury to virtue: I
' hate to be witty on an immoral sub-
' ject.'

' Few women, Henrietta, would
' mistake compliments for offences,
' and none be so severe upon them-
' selves. Words from those men's
' lips, like a trifling noise in a solitary
' place, can alarm or frighten but the
' fools and cowards. Wherever you
' go, you will meet the same men: all
' have desires, and will tell you of
' them; they differ only in the manner
' and expression. The audacity of a
' beau, and the respectful homage of a
' man diffident of his merit, are adapted
' to their characters; both talk as they
' feel, and behave as they dare. For-
' give mankind their errors; but take
' care not to be their victim. Like
' you, I want to breathe: let's go.'

LETTER XXIII.

THE woman of gallantry rejoices no more at the vain attempts of her jealous husband to surprize her upon the bed of guilt, and a prime minister at having secured a majority in his favour in both houses, than I did when I left Lady B——y's rout. My heart, free from constraint, dilated with inexpressible delight at the recovery of it's liberty. Like the light which dispels the fears of a child trembling in the dark, and gives him back the favourite toy he had lost, the freedom I enjoyed obliterated the odious hours, during which my mind had been the slave of fashion, and endeared to my senses the memory of Mr. Romney.

No longer did I suffer pride to sway over love, and fancy to impose upon my reason. The blind which the glitter-
ing

ing apparatus of grandeur, and the counsels of my mother, had put on my eyes, vanished as soon as I began to reflect. When in the cool hours of retirement, the soul being not then biassed by the presence of the delusive objects which attracted her attention, we appeal to our understanding from the judgment of our passions, how different the consequence we draw, the sentence we decree! At those hours, the ambitious, the miser, the voluptuous, and the lover, may see as clearly in their hearts, as they behold their features in a faithful glass. The vanity of their pursuits, and the ridicule of their wishes, are written in large characters before them; yet, though all have the power to read, how few will or can exert it! We are so averse to be enlightened, so unwilling to sacrifice errors to truth, that it would seem we are, from the moment we are born, put under the guard of folly. Reason, Reason! I am afraid thou art but an empty name! I see Ambition conquer Love, and Love conquer Avarice; but what passion ever yielded to the cool voice of Reason! That man is feebly affected whose soul can be easily argued into moderation; whose feelings, like the airs of a coquette, are at the command of his judgment.

LETTER XXIV.

SO apt is our mind to change and pass from one determination to another, that, unless the heart be absolutely taken up with a sensation, none can flatter themselves to welcome, the next day, the opinion they had the day before: such a fickleness is the satire of the modern education. If, at a time when our understanding may be modified at the pleasure of our instructors, we were not, through their ignorance, led into a false knowledge of the foibles of humanity, we would not labour under the mortal pang of suspense: our choices would be as unalterable as the fervour of a devotee, fully convinced of the existence and power of the God he adores. Some boast their constancy when once resolved; I believe them no more than I would a criminal, who pleads not guilty, in hope his guilt shall not be detected.

I was the next morning wavering still between love and pride, when the unexpected presence of Mr. Romney gave the victory to the former.

Mrs. Verman being not at home, I knew not at first whether I should receive him; but my heart talking in his favour, he was introduced.

My countenance did not bespeak the proud Henrietta; my sight had, however, such an effect upon him as to make his bow and his compliment extremely ungraceful and unmeaning.

'This man,' said I to myself, 'knows how to flatter: his confusion 'tells his respect; I must reward him 'for it.'

And I immediately called his spirits to order, by assuring, with a smile, I was pleased to see him.

'Oh! say again you are pleased!'

'What sense do you give to these 'words, that you wish to hear them re-'peated?'

'They have such a charm as to 'strike my soul with unspeakable de-'light! Forgive—but—Oh! Miss 'Henrietta, would this heart could 'lay open before you!'

'I am quite a stranger to the lan-'guage of a heart: I beg you would 'speak in a tongue I may understand 'and answer. How does Lady Ben-'net?'

And I sat down.

'Very well.'

And, with a sigh, he drew a chair near me.

'This opportunity I have long de-'sired for. Frown not; my happiness 'depends wholly upon your smiles. 'Beggar me not of this minute of bliss; 'my honesty has a friend in your vir-'tue. A true love can never give of-'fence; it is an homage due to beau-'ty.'

I had not the heart, Susannah, to play the coquette, and plague the man whose sincerity I could not question.

'I thought, Sir, you esteemed me 'too much to talk to my pride rather 'than to my reason. Do you believe 'me so void of sense as not to be able 'to hear but of flattery? What a mise-'rable opinion they entertain of the 'young women in this polite age! 'Pray, Sir, find another topick than 'my own person, or give me leave to 'retire. I am too proud to stay with 'a man who compliments my vanity at 'the expence of my character.'

'Mistake

'Mistake me not: I both esteem and love you. I have, undoubtedly, many of the faults peculiar to my age; but I detest falshood. Never have my lips belied my heart, and betrayed a virtuous woman into the belief of a passion I did not feel.'

'These are the very looks, the very expressions of deceit; all use them to betray.'

'In me they are the interpreters of truth.'

'If the most experienced women are daily dupes to the arts of men, what innocent maid is able to distinguish it from nature, and be free from doubt and fear! Imprudence and self-sufficiency may easily believe, and trust their charms for the security of a man's words. So long as I am not a fool, for me probability will not be conviction.'

'Will not you make an exception?'

'In your favour?'

'Indeed, I deserve it.'

'I have but your word; and you are a man.'

'Do you take me for an enemy?'

'No; but I will act as if you were.'

'So suspicious, and you live happy!'

'For that very reason I am not miserable.'

'What charms are there in insensibility?'

'Those of being safe from the pains of repentance.'

'How can you feel those when united to a man of honour?'

'The scarcity of such a character is not a temptation to credit it's reality.'

'How severe your satire of mankind! what, not one man of true merit?'

'What do you understand by true merit? I never heard of any thing so much spoken of; but it is so differently defined, that one would be apt to think it does not exist.'

'True merit consists in never doing or talking against the dictates of one's heart.'

'You frighten me. What! an avowed libertinism is the character of true merit! Who would not be a plague to society, were he to obey but the calls of his passions?'

'The natural depravity of our hearts, charming Henrietta, is corrected by an excellent education. A man of liberal principles is humane, generous, indulgent to all men, and severe only to himself.'

'But, Sir, the courtier's creed is absolutely the reverse of yours. You do not pretend, surely, to a greater degree of wisdom, which of you is right?'

'I appeal to your heart for a judgment between us.'

'I pronounce in your favour.'

He took my hand to his lips, and printed a kiss upon it.

'What avails my decision, if I favoured only a chimera? Where is the man resembling your description? By what signs may I know him from his mimick? Buffoons excel often in the parts they imitate. Think of the dangers to which one error exposes us, of the unavoidable humiliation attending our credulity; who will reflect, and not suspend his judgment, not wait till our reason satisfied objects no longer to the choice we make?'

'Too many cautions, Miss, are the poison of life: we should be the most wretched of all creatures, were our hearts in a perpetual calm, our minds ever capable of reflection. No pleasures could we enjoy, were we to submit them to the tribunal of reason. Who would venture on the perilous sea of marriage with the view of the storms impending upon it? What society would long subsist, were every individual to entertain a mutual diffidence one of another? I do not say, Miss, we should trust a man upon his apparent behaviour; too often is the shape of a man of honour the form of a rogue; but let this never keep so strict a guard upon himself, nature will betray him: if he has vices, he will forget himself, and be then the sport of our sex, and the scorn of yours. I am a man, therefore liable to imperfections and folly: this is no reason why I should be tainted with them. Let my actions, Miss, answer for my veracity; esteem me so long as I shall deserve it.'

'And you think, Sir, that a man cannot watch so attentively upon himself, as to keep incog. whilst he is pleased to be so?'

'Actuated by a strong passion, and in the hope of obtaining the prize he

D 'covets,

'covets, the ambitious may sacrifice nature to the only want he feels. But a real lover has constantly his heart on his lips; his soul is seen in his eyes; he has not the power to deceive. Respect is the characteristick of a lover; never will he, or can he, offend the object he is enamoured with.'

'And you love me?'

'The doubt is torment. I love, sincerely love you.'

And he fell on his knees.

'That your suspicions may entirely vanish, here is my hand; dispose of it. Do you still doubt my sincerity?'

I felt such a pleasure on seeing him at my feet, that I forgot to bid him to rise. Both my hands were in his; and my looks told him plainly I had a mind to believe.

'Do you still doubt my sincerity?'

'I do not. But——'

'But——'

How expressive of fear was his stammering of that word!

'You may change.'

'Change! No; never, never. I am happy——'

At that instant the door flew open, and my mother entered the room.

LETTER XXV.

'WHAT! Mr. Romney at my daughter's feet! at a first visit! What am I to believe?'

'Look upon her, Madam: was not my situation very natural? Who could with impunity behold such charms? I had a heart; it felt their power. My fortune and my hands are at her commands.—Dear Henrietta, your confusion is an affront upon your mother and me. Since she loves you, she cannot be offended at the respectful attachment of a friend of her family: my character and riches are as unquestionable as your beauty, and her affection for you. See our pardon in her looks.'

'I own, Sir, that I was surprized at the novelty. I did not, indeed I did not expect it; but I am not angry.'

These last words she spoke with a smile, and then darted at me an eye filled with indignation. She came to

'Is it thus, Miss, you keep the promise you made?'

'There is my excuse, Madam.'

And I pointed to Mr. Romney. The energy of my answer, still enforced by the firmness of my voice, confounded Mrs. Verman.

'He your excuse!'

She bit her lips with resentment, and went from me.

My mother had too much power over her passions not to subdue them instantly, when their knowledge would have submitted her to censure; and too much art, not to put the most obstinate man out of his favourite subjects, and give a conversation the turn she liked the best.

In vain did Mr. Romney seize every opportunity to introduce the topicks of love and marriage, his ingenuity was as often defeated by her prudence. Tired at last not to be able to put one word or two in favour of his desires, he took his leave, fully convinced that if he had my consent, he could not flatter himself with that of my mother.

LETTER XXVI.

SOON after Mr. Romney's retreat, Mrs. Verman's political indifference dwindled into a downright anger. Her sacrifice of this passion made it but the fiercer when she could indulge it. The bad man is not so heartily incensed at the honours conferred upon his enemy, as she was at the thought her reason had been the sport of my hypocrisy. Her offended pride made her for some time forget the miscarriage of her favourite plan. She could not bear having been the fool of a daughter, whose inclinations she fancied to have at her disposal. To see me act contrarily to her expectation, was an assault on her judgment she could not forgive. All this she expressed with looks, motions, and words. No longer was I her beloved Henrietta; but a base, ungrateful, unnatural wretch, whom she had nursed up like a tender friend, to be the most effectually robbed of her happiness, and stabbed to the heart.

Conscious I had not done any thing I ought to repent or blush for, I sat silent, and with all the intrepidity of innocence. The calm of my spirits raised her passion to a higher degree.

My

My insensibility of her wrongs was a keener injury than my dissimulation: this might be the effect of fear; but the former could only be caused by indifference or hatred.

Had I then attempted my defence, like the pilot who would sail against the tide and wind, the utmost efforts of art and ingenuity would have proved unsuccessful. As well might I have told a young widow, enchanted at the death of an abhorred husband, she should regret his loss, and be a prey to sorrow, than to have hoped to convince my mother of the reasonableness of my attachment to Mr. Romney, and the absurdity of her charge against me. I waited till she had absolutely lost the power of speech, and of expressing in her features a violent affection of the soul. So uncommon a flood of fury could not continue: the delicacy of her frame could not long labour under the destroying sensation: the moment came, when, between a half breathing and fainting, she forcibly abandoned to me her ears and her reason.

I told her of the force of the circumstances; she shook her head with contempt of the good qualities and fortune of Mr. Romney, which would satisfy even the ambition or sensibility of a girl my superior in birth or accomplishments.

'Weak girl! weak girl!'

And she put her hands upon her eyes.

'What happiness, dear Madam, can
' your daughter promise herself with
' a nobleman who will love her but
' so long as her charms shall please his
' fancy, and scorn her from the hour
' the novelty being vanished, he will
' repent the choice he made? Love may
' for a while silence pride and ambi-
' tion; but when it's illusions are pas-
' sed, will not the once favourite in-
' clination be cursed as the cause of
' endless shame and sorrow? If the
' good-nature of an husband does not
' permit him to declare his thoughts
' openly, does not the discerning self-
' love of his wife trace them in his be-
' haviour? What woman of any de-
' licacy can tamely suffer the dislike of
' her husband? Dislike! rather should
' I have said his contempt! What vir-
' tue can then be guarded against the
' temptation of revenge? Though a
' crime, who will not commit it? In
' vain should we call to religion for
' help against the resentment of our
' hearts. The woman, I fear, is al-
' ways between God and our prayers.
' Expose me not, dear Madam, to a
' futurity marked with despair, vice,
' and folly, In an union with Mr.
' Romney, equality of rank frees me
' from his disdain.'

'Leave me! leave me, thou thought-
' less girl!'

'I will not till I have found my mo-
' ther again.'

'Forget that man, and I am thy
' mother.'

'Would you see me miserable?'

'Thou art a fool, Henrietta; thou
' art a fool! Leave me.'

'On my knees I beg for forgiveness,
' and your approbation.'

'Expect neither of them. What ob-
' stinacy! I have no patience.'

And rising with the motions of the utmost displeasure.'

'To your room—no more will I
' hear—to your room this moment!'

I sighed, and obeyed.

LETTER XXVII.

THE two following days I was kept close prisoner, and forbid the use of my pen. This severity strengthened the passion it was intended to destroy. In the absence of the daily diversions which took up my time and my thoughts, my fancy naturally gave way to the feelings of my heart, as the sole relief against the tediousness of captivity. A perpetual reverie on the man we love must necessarily add to his charms, and our tenderness. He is not like a castle we build in the air with the richest materials our imaginations can dream of; and whose structure, in the sobriety of our senses, reason disapproves, and pulls down: this is not the fate of a lover; we are always so smitten with the agreeable picture, as to have it not in our power to discern it's defects. Mrs. Verman's proceedings favoured Mr. Romney: not once did Reason whisper that prejudice might lead the pencil. I drew, and was pleased with my work.

To these two days of entire solitude, Susannah, I owe my present misfortunes; they decided my passion, and made me the wretch I am. My mother—

ther—but that character is sacred—I must suppress my complaints, and suffer in silence.

* *

I was musing upon the continual divorces among the great, all caused either by an inequality of birth and fortune, or a difference of humour, and trembling to rank one day with these unfortunate; when the housekeeper gave me the following letter.

'TO MISS HENRIETTA VERMAN.

'WHEN my Henrietta's ingenuity, betraying the sentiments of her heart, opened before me the ever-flowery path of happiness, how could I have thought I was then upon the very brink of misery! I had hardly indulged the hope of bliss when it vanished, and left but pain behind. The starving wretch who, finding a purse of gold, is robbed of it at the very minute his soul dilates with joy at the delightful sight, suffers not half the torments my fatal disappointment has oppressed me with! Chance may still favour him; that is a comfort: I have none! Despair only is in view; it reaches my heart; it is torn—exquisitely torn! I wish but for death, since I cannot obtain my Henrietta!

'Mrs. Verman's ambition is an obstacle I have it not in my power to conquer. Of all passions it is the most inflexible; it hardens a heart, and beggars it of justice and humanity. Maternal love is now a dormant virtue in a mother's breast: of fancy or pride she obeys the dictates; they are the sole counsellors she advises with, either for the fashion of her dress, or the establishment of her children. This indifference of their happiness, once grown into habit, reason can never alter: she will have them see through her own eyes, argue as she feels, and conclude as she resolves. Oh, dear Henrietta! what have not I to fear? Who will soften Mrs. Verman into a compliance with our desires, if she commands, and will not leave to her daughter the liberty of her choice? Will not your virtue sacrifice the man of your heart to your mother; yield to her intreaties, or be compelled to obey, from the apprehensions of making her unhappy? This thought makes me mad! No! virtue orders not the inhuman sacrifice! You may disobey, and be still virtuous. The rights of a mother extend not to the power of making her children miserable. Both nature and law are in your favour, dear Henrietta: you have yourself rights which a mother can neither dispute nor invalidate; they are as sacred as hers. If you love me, your soul will be as free from her usurped authority as your choice: forgive, if I say it will be free from blame. Riches I ask not; your own person is the only portion I am desirous to possess. My passion is as disinterested as your virtues are real and unspotted: you only I love; any other advantage which your fortune can bestow I disdain; let Mrs. Verman enjoy it. Would it could pay for her consent! But, alas! her only foible is pride; and this, not gold, but titles and grandeur, can flatter and delight. Henrietta! how warmly she desired Lady Bennet yesterday to use all her influence over me, that I should no more think of you, as she was absolutely determined never to accept me for her son-in-law! As warmly did my aunt defend my cause. Had she spoke to a mother, we had gained: but the ambitious woman is not so easily subdued; her pleasure is her reason. Henrietta! dear Henrietta! from your generosity my tortured soul expects relief: pity a man whose sole crime is to love you; and not repent, though death should be the consequence of the passion he feels! One word from you will save me from destruction, and animate my courage to triumph over the obstinacy of pride and ambition. Oh! write that word; and I shall be yours,

'ROMNEY.

'P. S. Mrs. Verman's housekeeper will deliver you this letter: you may trust her with your answer. Henrietta! welcome the tears this paper will tell you I have shed: they are the tears of love and despair; welcome them! Adieu!'

LETTER

LETTER XXVIII.

'THOU shalt neither die nor despair!' exclaimed I, when I had read: 'my hand is a debt I must and will pay to thy love and generosity! Honour and virtue cannot object to thee for my husband: when these secure me the esteem of mankind, I will defend my lawful titles to freedom and happiness. Religion forbids suicide and falshood: would not my marrying the man I should hate be the murder of myself? and the Yes I should pronounce a wilful perjury? My soul scorns the constraint imposed upon it's affections. Thou lovest me! I shall be thine! For thee I will brave prayers and threatenings; I will not know the mother under the shape of a tyrant, and submit to her despotick sway!'

The last words were still on my lips, when I received Mrs. Verman's orders to step to her closet.

The chearful features she had put on cheated me not of my reason. My knowledge of her thoughts told me of a scene in which her heart and her tongue would be at a perpetual variance.

The awful gravity of my countenance announcing plainly that I was not happy, Mrs. Verman seemed to feel a concern, and to indulge a look of real tenderness. She made me a sign to take a chair and sit by her; then arose, and walked pensive, varying her motions according to the ascendancy which maternal love or indignation obtained in her mind. The latter at last prevailed; but, that it might not enforce my disobedience by provoking the haughtiness of my already incensed soul, she borrowed the mien and language of the former.

'When I condemned you to a few days retreat, Henrietta, I deprived myself of a daughter whose company and conversation are my delight. This apparent severity my attachment to you commanded: however painful the sacrifice, I hesitated not, since I hoped it would avail to your happiness.'

Here she smiled upon me; and, taking affectionately my hands in hers—

'I knew that the reason of my daughter would exert itself in the calm of a solitude, and reconcile her to the desires of a mother who, divested of every prejudice, free from the blindness of passion, sees things such as they are, and lives but to make you happy. Were not I swayed by this motive, my consent would instantly follow your inclination: with you would I think of the present only, forget the fatal effects of an indiscreet prepossession, and make no use of my experience.

'Were you certain, which is impossible, to love, and be loved, till age, deadening desire, puts a period to enjoyment, I would still tell you, Henrietta, you shall be unhappy. If your heart feels passions your husband cannot gratify, the days you shall live will be a perpetual transition from pain to pleasure; and this, though ever so exquisite, will yield to the keenness of the former. Unless you are absolutely divested of pride, envy, ambition, and avarice, I tell you again, you shall be unhappy. But you are a woman, Henrietta; therefore liable to change, to feel, and be deceived. It is with pleasure as with our taste for plays, musick, and dancing. Who long like the repetition of the same amusements? do they not leave our soul in a vacuity of sensations, although in the midst of their pretended raptures?

'Innumerable are our wants, Henrietta; their chain is linked up from a real passion to the seemingly insignificant caprice: each has a poignancy which brooks no privation; it is a torment to wish in vain for the satisfaction of a desire. You have none now but to please Mr. Romney; but to think he loves you: you shall have the same so long as I attempt to destroy it. Such is the effect of a contradicted passion; but does not your reason tell you that this very desire subsists only from my opposition, and that my consent would presently weaken it in your heart? Through your own obstinacy, would you be deaf to your own interest, and engage in a marriage of which you must and shall repent one day? Love is like champaign; it pleases the taste, and intoxicates the understanding. Who, from a thousand instances, convinced it has such an effect, will trust only to experience for the certainty of it,

'or

'or drink it immoderately, or not re-
'move the obnoxious bottle from his
'fight? As the palate is at last dif-
'gusted at the bewitching liquor, so
'does any passion whatever die away
'in the heart of a woman. I except
'none but pride, the ever-faithful
'companion of self-love; which at all
'times, and every season of life, con-
'tinues to command, and to be
'obeyed.'

LETTER XXIX.

'MADAM! Madam!——'
And I gave my head the impatient turn of incredulity.

The solemn dignity of my exclamation, and the sense I marked it with, astonished my mother.

'Will not religion and virtue secure
'my peace and felicity better than the
'power of gratifying every call of a
'depraved fancy? You talk of pride
'and self-love as the supreme rulers of
'our actions: what would religion and
'virtue avail mankind, were they, far
'from obeying, authorized to violate
'their dictates? The man who could
'erase from his mind the ideas of just
'and unjust, and adopt his pleasure
'for his only law, would forfeit his
'nature, and be a monster. My at-
'tachment to Mr. Romney, supported
'by the love of my duty, will enable
'me to reach, with honour, the career
'I have to run over. Were I to travel
'it with a man whose only merit should
'be his coronet, the spectators, under
'the attire of content, would see in me
'the victim of vanity, here and there,
'in search of the happiness she had
'thoughtlessly lost.'

'Did you live in a community of
'nuns, your eloquence would make a
'very brilliant part in their enthusi-
'astick tittle-tattle. Poor Henrietta!
'how fallen thou art! I admire your
'morals, and compliment you upon
'your new-enlightened scruples: when
'indifferent, your reason was the envy
'of all your friends. You love; they
'are revenged: from their hearts they
'will pity you—indeed they will pity
'you! As I hope, however, that you
'are not beyond the power of remedy,
'I give you four and twenty hours to
'argue your senses into their usual
'coolness and sobriety. Abuse not

'your judgment; it will easily point
'out to you the means for a prompt
'recovery. If, then, your fit is not
'over, I will be the physician myself,
'and force a cure on your distempered
'brain. Since your reason is asleep,
'your mother's must be awakened, to
'save you from the dangers of infatua-
'tion: it is my duty, and I will dis-
'charge it. I know I have not your
'thanks for being so studious of your
'happiness; that your heart rebels
'against the method I take to procure
'it to you: your ingratitude offends
'me not. As I would not ask a blind
'man his opinion of the dress I wear,
'in the circumstance you are, I will
'not require you should be just or able
'to distinguish the remedy from the
'poison: to me it belongs to take care
'you should not mistake.'

And, with a nod of her head, she bid me to retire.

LETTER XXX.

'HEIGH-HO!' sighed I, when
I had got into my room; and I leaned a few minutes upon the back of a chair: my heart so oppressed, yet unable to relieve it by the shedding of one single tear.

'Is it possible,' exclaimed I, with the mournful accent of sorrow, 'that
'the passion I feel should be only a
'whim which rises and dies in our
'breasts as fancy commands! that,
'from my mother's mere opposition to
'my wishes, Mr. Romney borrows his
'merit, and I indulge my hopes of
'happiness! If so, of what use to us
'can Reason be? Why does she deny
'me the help she grants to my mother?
'How came I, though willing, not to
'part a chimera from reality? I feel I
'love; every thought confirms it: yet
'I love not! Ridiculous! I am not so
'much under the sway of folly as to
'be guilty of so unreasonable a mis-
'take! I love; and Mr. Romney is
'the object!'

I sat down, and took the letter he had written; read it again and again; and every perusal added to my esteem and love for him.

'My mother differs from me, and
'objects to my choice!' The thought filled my heart with vexation. 'The
'hatred of a mother!' My soul, Su-
sannah,

fannah, sunk under the fear of that hatred. I was instantly bedewed with tears, and murmured half an hour against the rigour of my fate, which had placed the displeasure of a mother between happiness and me.

※ ※

Mrs. Moulton, the housekeeper, found me dejected, and in the utmost despondency, when she came into the room. The spectacle of my sorrow drew sobbings from her bosom, and tears from her eyes: she respected my silence, and partook of my agony.

'Dear Mrs. Moulton!—my mother —my mother! I have no hopes—I am miserable!—She hates the thought of Mr. Romney!—Oh! my heart bursts with pain!—She threatens—Mrs. Moulton—she has threatened me!— But four and twenty hours has she granted to my reason for the conquest of my passion! Then, if I continue to love, from her I am to expect hatred and ill usage—from a mother!— who can endure the fatal stroke!— from a mother! My virtue is shocked—her anger will be death!'

'Your respect for your mother, Miss, I will not weaken: I will spare your delicacy my judgment of her behaviour. However uncommonly severe, however contrary to the feelings of a tender parent, you are her daughter; I shall not, against her, vindicate your wrongs: but is she to abuse the authority your good-nature gives her over you; to turn to your disadvantage an attachment she should reward, and overlook your happiness, to gratify a whim? The rights of a mother end when she begins to be unjust: no longer can children be compelled to obey, or fear the sting of remorse for a rebellion which nature avows. The sacrifice of one's self all laws disapprove; that folly can enter the heads only of the fools and mad. Mr. Romney will justify your disobedience: malice or envy have no darts to throw against him, so real are his virtues and fortune. Your mother herself will not dare to shew an indignation she could not support: although vexed at the miscarriage of a project her pride had delighted to form, her respect for herself will smother it in her breast; her pride itself will force her to applaud what she condemns in her heart. Be no longer uneasy, dear Miss; relieve that oppressed heart with the hope of being happy; the man you love you shall have: let this trickling tear be the last you shed.'

'Mrs. Moulton, if my mother could forgive, think of the interval between her anger and her pardon! her sufferings my soul will partake. Mr. Romney's smiles, and unfeigned affection, will not make me unnatural; still I shall be a daughter, though forsaken by my mother.'

'That situation will be but short: what are a few days of trouble to years of real misery? Would you marry a man you should hate, in compliment to Mrs. Verman's choice?'

'Talk not thus! Never would I! So much baseness my soul disdains!'

'Then you must be certain to live at a perpetual enmity with her. Does not her refusal of Mr. Romney prove her partiality to another? You know him not yet; but to-morrow—next week—his hand may be tendered to you with the voice of absolute command. Perhaps a man, exhausted by age and debauchery, without any virtues to commend him to your esteem but the fictitious honours he inherited from his ancestors: you shudder; the picture may be realized. False pride is always easily contented; it grasps at a shadow; a brilliant nothing will satisfy it!'

'You frighten me! What can I do?'

'Of two evils chuse the least. Put in one scale your love for Mr. Romney, with the transitory anger of Mrs. Verman; and, in the other, twenty years of an incessant dislike and sorrow: weigh well; which will carry it?'

'My love! my love! No longer am I in suspense; no longer will I trust my happiness to the discretion of a prepossessed mother! Was she insensible of the evils she exposes me to, of the error she so tenderly cherishes, and sincerely wishing to discover her mistake, I might flatter myself to open her mind to the light of reason, and be happy with her own consent. Even then, as her denial would proceed from her affection to me, I should wait till every fear should be subsided, every doubt lost in conviction: but Mrs. Verman cannot be
'deceived;

'deceived; she loves me not; herself,
and not me, she considers in the disposal of my hand. Like the volup-
tuary, who, scorning to please the
taste of his guests, orders his dinner
to his own liking, regardless of my
inclinations, she would force upon
me the man of her fancy. She is my
mother: can the name make up for
the want of tenderness, and bind me,
like the slave, to have no will to think
but at the pleasure of a tyrant? No! I
shake off the disgraceful yoke, and will
be myself. Scruples, away! too long
have I laboured under your delusion:
I will love, and be free.—Dear Mrs.
Moulton, let Mr. Romney be acquainted with the sentiments of my
heart; let him know he pleases, and
I will be his: from me he deserves
the flattering assurance. Tell him I
am sensible of his love and merit;
tell him—but no—he asks a word—
I will write it—fetch me paper and
pen—I have been unmercifully de-
barred of their use. Go! make haste!
I will hear nothing! My soul is impatient of delay! my lover must be
happy! Who knows but this very
minute he curses the air he breathes?
Oh! let him not blaspheme against a
life I will have him to enjoy! Go!
Why do you stare? Have not you
heard me?'

My enthusiasm, Susannah, had passed in Mrs. Moulton's heart; her joy
at my sudden resolve had taken from
her the powers of speech and motion;
twice I repeated the order before I perceived she was unable to obey.

Alarmed at her silence, still more at
her frightful stupid countenance, I
shook her by her hand; down upon the
floor came the staring, open-mouthed
Mrs. Moulton. Her fall restored immediately their activity to her inani-
mated senses.

'Lord! Lord! I was so struck!
How happy Mr. Romney! What
news for him!'

And she half limped, half ran out of
the room for the materials I wanted.

'VIRTUE cannot be offended,' exclaimed I when alone: 'it is not a false
step. I may, without blushing, own
the passion of my heart to the man
who feels the same for me: coquetry
may think it prudent to be false. I
love; I will be true: it is criminal
to play with the happiness of the man
we really believe sincere and deserving.'

'He is so; he is so: I answer for
him,' said Mrs. Moulton, who had
heard the last phrase.

'Have not I a better guarantee than
your word?'

And I smiled.

'You have it in your charms.'

'Flatterer!'

I sat down, and wrote the following
letter.

* *

'TO CHARLES ROMNEY, ESQUIRE.

'SIR,

'I Have searched into my heart, and
found I esteem you; nay, there
often a more tender sentiment than
esteem prevails: did modesty give me
leave, I would name it love. My
consciousness of your virtues keeps me
from blotting out the word. I have
written it; you may read. I love; I
will not deny it: but of what avail
is my telling I love you to our happiness? A mother!—I will write no
more.

'HENRIETTA VERMAN.'

LETTER XXXI.

AFTER the step I had taken, Susannah, neither my mind nor my
heart could change, and tamely suffer
the tyranny of a mother. From the
conviction that my character was, and
would be free from slander, I grew
strong and unconquerable.

The return of Mrs. Moulton, on
whose features wandered the talkative
joy of a successful messenger, and the
sight of a letter from Mr. Romney, increased still my courage, and assured
my triumph.

Mrs. Moulton would have made
sport with my impatience; but, however agreeable to hear, I could not then
listen. From her I snatched the letter,
broke the seal open, and involuntarily
kissed the first line my eyes fell upon.

'TO MISS HENRIETTA VERMAN.

'YOU love me! Welcome to my
' heart are the rapturous words.
' You love me! My soul has passed in
' my eyes to read the enchanting ex-
' pression, to intoxicate itself with de-
' light at the unexpected bliss. You
' love me! No longer am I fearful; I
' brave every obstacle, and defy the most
' inveterate enemy! Oh, Henrietta!
' you have restored life to my dying
' spirits: this life is your work; it is,
' and ever shall be devoted to you! every
' thought, every desire shall center in
' you! I will think but to please! I will
' wish but to see you happy! Not once
' shall you perceive an abatement in my
' affection, in my transports! Ever eager
' to gaze, to listen, to enjoy, my feelings
' will have the constant fire of novelty.
' What luxuriancy of raptures your
' possession flatters me with! Each sense
' alternately, all sometimes at once will
' sink under the load of pleasure: you
' will satisfy their restless curiosity, and
' fix them upon your looks, your mo-
' tions, your words; and, under your
' heavenly touch, my happiness will be
' too exquisite; it will be more than a
' mortal can bear. You love me!
' How many the pleasing emotions
' springing from these words! A par-
' don is not more grateful to the cri-
' minal condemned to die, than these
' words are to my heart. You love
' me! you have made me a man. Mrs.
' Verman, though never so inflexible,
' shall yield; she cannot resist the en-
' treaties of a lover: if she does, I
' have a friend, a powerful friend, in
' your heart. Henrietta! listen to his
' counsels, he shall not deceive you!
' my honour warrants the resolution
' you will form! From me dread no-
' thing but an excess of love! I will
' expect passion for passion! a flame as
' fierce as mine! I should be unhappy,
' did not I see in your eyes the same
' sensibility my own will perpetually
' betray. Try well thy heart, Hen-
' rietta; and then hesitate not to trust
' thy happiness to my care: thou shalt
' walk upon the flowers of life; it's
' thorns I will conceal from thee.

'ROMNEY.'

LETTER XXXII.

'HOW rapturous he writes, Mrs.
'   Moulton! How forcible this
' letter!'
' You have still added to it's energy
' by your manner of reading it. Had
' Mr. Romney heard you, he would
' have mistaken your soul for his. It
' were a pity two such feeling hearts
' should be parted; they must not, they
' shall not, be parted.'
' God only can tear him from my
' heart! I love, I love! I am beyond the
' power of a mortal physician! My at-
' tachment to my mother will not avail
' her! It fights not upon equal terms
' with my love! This sways entirely
' over my heart! No room is there in
' it for the authority of a mother! No
' other law but it's own can I acknow-
' ledge and obey!'
' The sentiments of Mr. Romney
' you have echoed. Thus he feels,
' thus he expresses himself, dear crea-
' ture! Would you had seen him af-
' ter he had perused your letter! He
' frightened me out of my wits; joy
' made him absolutely mad: how he
' talked and skipped about! I was nigh
' ringing for the servants to come up.
' He minded me no more than if he
' had had no witness of his folly; but
' went on chattering the most strange
' things, and kissing the comforting
' paper, thus he called it. Poor man!
' Oh! he loves you dearly. When he
' came to himself—" What! are you
" there, Mrs. Moulton? You have
" brought me life." And he kissed
' the letter again and again. Then he
' sat down; and the—" You love me!"
' was ten times on his lips for once he
' traced it upon the paper. His heart
' was full; the answer was soon writ-
' ten.
" Tell my dear Henrietta, that she
" has made me the happiest from the
" most wretched of mankind. Tell
" her I am at her absolute disposal;
" that she may, at her pleasure, com-
" mand my fortune and my hand;
" that no heart ever felt a more sin-
" cere passion. Oh! Mrs. Moul-
" ton—"
' Here the word expired on his
'tongue,

'tongue; he breathed one sigh. I discovered the trickling tear in his eyes. Like him I was affected, trembling, out of breath. What more moving than an handsome young man shedding a tear! though from joy it is a pain; my soul partook of it.'

"Your sensibility, dear Mrs. Moulton, is an omen I welcome; it proves to me, you will be faithful to the interests of two lovers who stand in need of your help: a tender woman can never be false. Tell Henrietta to trust to my probity; that whatever partiality she may favour me with, she never shall repent of it. I long to see her; but how, when, or where, I know not: from her generosity I expect that pleasure; all my attempts, all my ingenuity, could not procure it me. The orders Mrs. Verman has given against me are too positive not to be punctually obeyed. Besides, could I get admittance, I might be betrayed; and my Henrietta would be the sufferer. I cannot think to give her one minute of uneasiness. Our indiscretion would infallibly raise her mother's anger, and perhaps exasperate her beyond the hope of forgiveness. Possibly I am too prudent; but I really love: and, since my Henrietta's virtue pleads still for her mother's rights, I would obtain her hand but when her soul shall feel no other sensations than those of joy. Sorrow in my Henrietta's breast would cause one sigh in the midst of our endearments, and poison all the transports of love. If Mrs. Verman's inflexibility continues, then, conscious of having done her duty, Henrietta will come to my arms, without one motive for a tear; then our life shall be a continual scene of bliss: let us, for a few days, a few weeks, respect Mrs. Verman's denial; no more time will my Henrietta grant, if she loves me; it is sufficient to satisfy her delicacy——"

'What! you weep, dear Miss?'

'I do; and with pleasure, at the knowledge you give me of Mr. Romney's sentiments. How should not I love the man who thinks so nobly? But pray go on, Mrs. Moulton.'

'Then he made me promise to contrive an unsuspected interview, where, in my presence, he might tell you of his love; and, putting this letter in my right-hand, he slid this ring into my left. I blushed, and would not receive it; but he himself put it upon this finger, and never would take it again.'

Forgive, Susannah, if I expatiate upon such a frivolous topick: at that time it delighted my soul; even now I remember it with pleasure.'

LETTER XXXIII.

THE next morning Mrs. Verman, mindful of her word, came up to my apartment. The two first hours of my rest had been taken up by love; the remaining nature had invaded. I was still in a sound sleep, when Mrs. Moulton drew the curtains, and announced my mother's visit.

'What! not yet up! Since Henrietta can rest, her mind must be composed. Was she yet wavering between her lover and me, her heart should be awaked: we do not enjoy sleep in the tumult of the passions. Have I then found my daughter again?'

And she passed her arm round my neck to embrace me.

'Stop, Madam: if tenderness is not the real spring of your caress, stop; I may not deserve it.'

'Is it possible your infatuation should last so long? No; your reason has got the better of a blind passion: you are my daughter; let me press you to my bosom; you are in tears! Henrietta, you will be the death of your mother.'

'To save one day of yours, dear Madam, I would give my whole life: far from me the thought of ever offending my mother! I love you with the utmost affection. Turn not your head from me: to that frown I have not been used; it is a mortal blow upon my sensibility. Why should we be miserable, when we can so easily be happy?'

And I respectfully carried her hand to my lips.

'Still silent, still an angry look at me! Is my attachment to Mr. Romney such a crime as not to be forgiven?'

'A new insult! How did you dare
' to

'to name him before me? The man I
detest!'

'What vice in him has provoked my mother? Nothing but the fear of my unhappiness could thus obliterate her generosity. Were he not really unworthy of me, my mother would be more indulgent.'

'His character I do not impeach; he may possess every virtue others boast to have, and have not: but I do not like the man who robs me of my daughter's affection; that guilt is unpardonable.'

'That guilt is only a chimera. None ever loved a mother as I do.'

'As you do! How false!'

'I am not false! God avert I should tell a lye to my mother!'

'Let your actions speak your attachment to me; they shall not, like words, impose upon my credulity: oppose me no longer in the only point I ever wished to carry. Forget Mr. Romney: to that test I put your veracity. What! no answer!'

'To prove my veracity, must I be guilty of falshood, belie my heart, and, to please you, dissemble it's real feelings? My mother ever taught me to respect myself. I will not feign; I love Mr. Romney!'

'Presumptuous girl! I hate you!'

She bit her lips, and stamped with her foot.

'Repeal! repeal the word! Curse not your daughter with your hatred!'

'I say it again; I hate you!'

And she flung herself out of the room, with the steps and motions of the most violent fury.

LETTER XXXIV.

'I Am hated by my mother! From her own lips I have heard she hates me!' Dear Susannah, my heart failed me; a cold fit seized upon every limb; I wished I could cease to love. The hatred of my mother, though unjust, struck my soul with terror; my spirits sunk under the weight of grief; I fainted in Mrs. Moulton's arms.

Her cries soon alarmed the whole house. 'Henrietta, the young, amiable Henrietta, is dying!' The dreadful news, passing from one servant to another, reached quickly Mrs. Verman's ear: she ran up with the utmost precipitation. At the sight of her daughter laying almost motionless upon the bed, despair animated instantly every feature; she stammered the most doleful complaints, and breathed the sobbings of real anguish. When I opened my eyes, I saw her by me bedewed with tears; a prey to the most poignant anxiety; too weak yet to rejoice at the unfeigned tenderness she forcibly expressed; to utter the gratitude I felt, my looks told her—'You do not hate me; nature has betrayed the mother!' She understood their language; but would not answer it. The certainty of my recovery changed her concern into a visible indifference: I no longer saw but Mrs. Verman; the mother was vanished.

* *

'She loves me; yet she will coldly see me miserable!' This thought incensed my heart against her, and allayed the flutter of my spirits: I got up, dressed, and was myself again.

'I will see Mr. Romney,' said I to Mrs. Moulton: 'but let prudence guide the step. I will not be exposed to the censure of the world: though it cannot disturb the peace of the innocent, it is, however, a disgrace they should avoid. It is not enough to be really virtuous, one must appear so; mankind are so inclined to slander and believe. Mrs. Moulton, Virtue herself would have the poisonous darts of calumny aimed at her, were she to come among us under her heavenly form. The severity of my mother will have a period: when I am free, either the play-houses, or the publick walks, will afford an opportunity; till then I cannot see him. I know I may go to church; Mrs. Verman's anger would readily yield to her duty: but rather would I die than to prophane, with the expressions of love, the sacred place of worship. This crime, though daily perpetrated, is no less odious—my heart abhors what my reason condemns!'

'But if your imprisonment is to last, what will become of Mr. Romney? He will die if he does not see you.'

'I will write.'

'A letter cannot compensate for the privation of your company: it has charms, it is true; but how weak compared to the pleasure of a conversation enlivened by a mutual love!

E 2 'Could

'Could you be contented with only hearing from him? You sigh; judge of his heart by your own. Would you have him suffer when you can relieve him?'

'How can I, Mrs. Moulton?'

'By recovering your liberty, and bestowing your hand upon him.'

'He shall have it: but let me first try to soften my mother; she may relent when convinced her opposition is vain.'

'If this hope is the praise of your virtue, it is not that of your discernment. The ambitious have an inflexibility which takes a new force from a spirited resistance: the conceit they are infatuated with, neither time nor reason can destroy. However, I may be wrong: far from me to dissuade you from making the attempt. Though now in a servile state, I have not forgot the virtues I practised in an happier situation. I approve your resolution, charming Henrietta: may it be attended with success!'

LETTER XXXV.

SUSANNAH! do not you love this Mrs. Moulton? She is no more: every day I shed one tear over her memory; every day I am sensible of her loss. Brought up in affluence, and reduced, by unmerited misfortunes, to the lowest ebb of misery, my mother took her into her house. Although she served, her soul was ever independent of her fortune: she continued to think freely, behave with dignity, and act with honour. The care she had taken of my infancy had endeared me to her: but though she looked upon me as her daughter, her impartiality always decided between my mother and me. For her against me when reason was on her side, for me against her when it turned the scale in my favour. Dear Mrs. Moulton! I will not stop the trickling tear; from me she deserves it.

* *

Two hours had slipped away imperceptibly in the enchanting tittle-tattle of love, when I heard the rattling of silk, and immediately saw Mrs. Verman. The freshness of my complection announcing I was well, she omitted the—'How-d'ye-do?' and sat by me.

'For the last time, Miss, I am come to eradicate from your mind the error you delight to indulge. Your enthusiasm is no wonder: at your season of life, it is in our nature to be the sport of the first passion we feel. Experience only can separate it's illusions from it's reality, by comparing the new sensations with the former effects the same had upon us. I pity your situation, as I do that of a fool or a lunatick: no more than they, at this minute, can you make use of your understanding: it is sunk below the power of reflecting. Perhaps it is folly in me to attempt to bring you back to reason: but I like to yield to my tenderness, which whispers, that my daughter's condition is not yet desperate. Yes, Henrietta, you are not yet so far gone as to render vain the remedy I will administer.

'No longer will I tell you that, in the short space of a few months, your affections may vary from love to indifference, and from indifference to hatred; that it is downright extravagance to believe in the continuance of a sensation, and still more stupid to found our happiness upon it. Our passions have the instability of the wind. What would your opinion be of a pilot, who sailing to the south with a fresh gale, thinking it not possible it could on a sudden shift to another point of the compass, would quietly fall asleep at the helm, and thus voluntarily expose himself to the danger of a shipwreck? You easily form a judgment of that man; yet, Henrietta, you will not see you deserve yourself from me the very sentence you pronounce against him.'

* *

'Out of the innumerable instances of the inconstancy and the power of the passions, I will give you but one. Suppose that jealousy should paint your lover to your fancy as unfaithful and perfidious: if that conceit grew inveterate in your mind, I tell you, Henrietta, that, influenced by pride, you would, out of spite, give your hand to his hated rival. What is that passion which a foolish whim can erase from your heart? Since you cannot doubt the probabi-
'lity

'lity of such a changement, are not
'you utterly convinced, that from our
'prepossession only a passion gathers all
'it's strength, and that it has therefore
'no reality? A child has fancied a
'wooden toy; offer him a gold one,
'he despises it: you are that child,
'Henrietta.'

Here my mother stopped to take breath, and search in my looks for the effect her speech had upon my heart. She saw but the satisfaction we necessarily feel when we hear a sensible orator. I wondered she could hope to silence a passion with words: however plausible the arguments she employed, they glanced only upon my mind; I continued to love.'

LETTER XXXVI.

AFTER a few minutes of a fruitless enquiry, Mrs. Verman went on in the following manner.

'I have a secret, Miss, which will
'perhaps cure the wound reason can-
'not heal: if your disease resists this
'remedy, I give you over. The Earl
'Osenvor loves you.'

'The Earl Osenvor! You amaze
'me!'

'He himself, Henrietta, is the man
'who was ambitious of deserving your
'hand; and to whom I destined it.'

'Never did he seem to distinguish
'me; never did he say he loved but
'with the accent of a flatterer! Of all
'the noblemen you could name, him
'I esteem the most; his visits always
'were welcome; to him, without dis-
'gust, I could listen; not once did he
'offend my modesty either with a look,
'or in expression: often have I com-
'mended the decency of his carriage.
'He is polite without affectation, witty
'without slander, virtuous without
'shame. Oh, Madam! you are too
'inhuman in your revenge! Indeed,
'indeed, you hate your daughter; you
'have pierced my heart with sorrow!
'Must the only man I looked upon as
'my friend, love me in vain? Why did
'not you keep the fatal secret? My
'knowledge of it is a new torment: I
'am unhappy!'

'Unhappy! when fortune offers you
'for a husband the man you esteem!'

'The man I esteem: but him I love

'not. If his passion for me is as sin-
'cere as mine for Mr. Romney, he
'must be miserable; my heart bleeds
'for him!'

'Soon he will return from the coun-
'try: there he went to terminate a
'family affair; thence he is to come
'to make, at your feet, the tender of
'his rank. How disappointed when
'he knows——'

'He shall know it from me, Ma-
'dam.'

'From you, Henrietta! Are you in
'earnest?'

'I am, Madam: I will not deceive
'the man I respect; it would be base
'to give him hopes I should know to
'be false. Since from me he could
'conceal his passion, it is not deeply
'rooted in his heart: mine I will trust
'to his generosity; he has too noble,
'too delicate a soul, to wish for an
'happiness I should not partake. A-
'gainst himself he will take the part of
'my lover; with you he will be our
'advocate.'

'And not gain his cause, were he
'such a fool.'

'What! would you still oppose,
'though he himself should abandon
'his rights?'

'Never, never will he part with
'them!'

'But if he does——'

'But if it should happen that you
'would not desire it?'

'Lord! it is impossible!

'How, then, can you expect he
'should be more generous than you?
'When you overlook his happiness,
'will he mind your own? Make not
'such dreams, Henrietta, when you
'are awake. What could give Lord
'Osenvor a power over his passion,
'which you are certain not to have
'over yours? I gave my word before
'you saw Mr. Romney: it is sacred;
'I shall not depart from it.'

'Then we all shall be miserable!'

'Then it will be your fault, and
'your fault only. Were his lordship's
'manners and morals really worthy
'of contempt, I would have scorned
'to enter into an alliance with him:
'but you are conscious of the con-
'trary; you are perfectly convinced
'he deserves you, your esteem speaks
'his merit. Henrietta, from esteem to
'love there is but one step.'

'Oh!

'Oh! my heart will burst with grief; I have no strength for such a load of vexations!'

'You know Lord Ofenvor; you know not Mr. Romney: your love for him is almost the work of enchantment. Like an unknown strong odour, which, carelessly smelt, at once overpowers every sense, his sight has operated upon your heart: it is but an illusion; Lord Ofenvor's presence will destroy it.'

'If it does not——'

'Well, then, I will not think of it; such an effect must necessarily follow.'

'Had you my heart, how differently you would conclude! You speak of infatuation; I am not under it's sway: I am very clear upon the nature of my attachment to Mr. Romney; it has sprung more from reflection than from my fancy; they have helped one another, and my soul has yielded to their united power.'

'How unfortunate Lord Ofenvor!'

'How unhappier I! He will have but his own sufferings, when I shall feel for yours and for his. Oh, Madam——'

And I fell at her feet.

'Pity your daughter! I love; and am not obstinate! I wish Lord Ofenvor were the man I love: to reconcile my affections with my duty would be a real bliss; but this is only a wish!'

The doleful tone of my voice, and some tears which dropped on her hand, seemed to affect sensibly my mother. I heard a smothered sobbing, and discovered a concern in the sudden and quick panting of her bosom: her looks flattered me with her forgiveness; I thought I saw the word upon her half-opened lip; my soul, between fear and joy, was upon the wing for it. Nature was once more sacrificed to ambition; the word was not pronounced. Afraid of betraying herself, my mother arose, passed her handkerchief over my eyes, and, after a tender kiss on my forehead, went away.

LETTER XXXVII.

THE sensibility my mother could not dissemble revived my heart, which had greatly suffered from the secret she had disclosed, and the scene that had ensued. Her choice of Lord Ofenvor proved her tenderness: had she only consulted her pride, neither my taste nor judgment would she have regarded; the old, infirm, and contemptible, would equally have had her approbation, so that her thirst for grandeur should have been satisfied. Had my soul been free, no objection could I have made. I really esteemed Lord Ofenvor; and, had he spoke when I could listen, I would have thought it a glory, an happiness, to deserve him: but he had not; and I loved when he would.

The offers of men of the same rank my mother had politely refused. Though she seemed not to watch my inclinations, she had perceived the preference I gave to Lord Ofenvor; and her heart had rejoiced at the possibility of gratifying both her favourite passion and her love for me. This new light on her behaviour silenced instantly the indignation it had forced into my breast; I felt a pang of sorrow for the injury I had done her, and sincerely repented of my injustice.

'I have no wrongs to complain of,' said I to myself: 'Mrs. Verman acted the mother when I thought her only ambitious and indifferent. With the world, her choice is her justification; to my eye, as she is perfectly acquainted with Lord Ofenvor's virtues, and my prejudice in his favour, her inflexibility is reason: her experience may foresee what I think it impossible ever to happen. "Try your heart well," writes Mr. Romney. I will; and if it continues to feel as it does now, all my mother's entreaties will not avail Lord Ofenvor: but then from her hands only will I receive my lover. This sacrifice gratitude commands; and I will make it.'

END OF THE FIRST VOLUME.

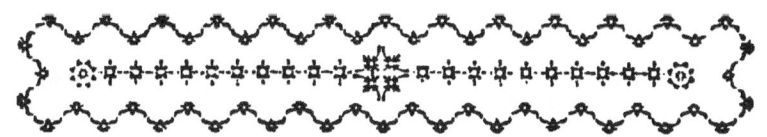

HENRIETTA,

COUNTESS OSENVOR.

VOLUME THE SECOND.

LETTER I.

HENRIETTA, COUNTESS OSENVOR,
TO LADY SUSANNAH FITZROY.

WHETHER Mrs. Verman thought that solitude was more her enemy than Mr. Romney, or she was apprehensive for my health, I know not; but I received an unexpected order to come down to dinner.

'I wish, Henrietta, I could find a talisman against the tyranny of the passions; they are the bane of pleasure! What a change a few days have made in our life! We were both so happy! Cursed for ever be the day I went with you to Lady Bennet! If I have lost the heart of my daughter, let me, however, see her in her countenance! I love you, I want to be deceived: this delusion I may one day repay!'

'Doubt no more my affection than you would my virtue.'

'Put on, then, a look of indifference instead of that loving one; I hate to see it; with the former the deception will be more natural. Who knows but, in mimicking, you may realize it? How often do not mankind take the spirit of the airs they assume? Very little of prepossession is capable of changing a character, or forming a new one: we all are children from the days we think not to those we boast to reason.

'Very few, at every season of life, have not a particular folly to indulge: like a child's bauble, our sensations have their day; this hour an enthusiast, the next an unbeliever. If, among the company I expect, one could read your thoughts, Henrietta, ten to one he would attract your attention, and divert you from Mr. Romney; and had he as much skill as knowledge, that Mr. Romney you are so fond of might to-morrow receive his congé coldly written with your own hands. You shake your head, and will not believe: like you I have been young, and had my opinion; like me, perhaps, an unforeseen incident will make you sensible of your error.'

* *

'I was not seventeen years old, when chance threw in my way a man exactly formed to turn a virgin's head: shape, features, wit, and talents, he united to a miracle. So much superior was he to any man I had seen before, that my heart, after a trifling defence, surrendered to it's conqueror. I thought but of him; dressed but for him; him only I condescended to please: his birth and fortune agreeing with mine, my pa-

'rents

'rents approved our passion, and granted my hand as soon as it was asked. The wedding-day was fixed. You may imagine, Henrietta, how happy I fancied myself! To marry the man I loved! it is the sole real bliss upon earth! I enjoyed it with the delirium of an intoxicated soul! Should, then, an angel have descended from Heaven, and told me—"You are deluded; you love not!" I would not have credited him.'

'An hour before the marriage articles were to be signed, I was amusing myself with a squirrel I liked, and feeding him with my own hands, when my lover entered the room. For a few minutes he partook of the innocent diversion, and helped the little animal to a bit of a nut: one kiss was his reward. On a sudden, my gentleman, very likely to try my temper, fell on the squirrel, and, before I could fly to his relief, wrested his neck, and killed him. This inhumanity presently beggared my lover of all his charms; I saw in him a monster, whose presence was a torment: so quickly did my inclination vanish, that I did not even deign to upbraid him with his cruelty!

'I rushed out of the room, and shut the door after me. My father was the first I met with as I ran down the stairs. The flutter of my spirits betrayed the inward emotion: he took me by the hand, pressed me to his bosom, and would absolutely know the cause. I could not speak: he led me to his closet; then a flood of tears relieved my oppressed heart. I began to breathe; and, falling on my knees, entreated him not to oppose the resolution I had just formed never to marry Mr. Morley. How amazed was my father! So sudden an indifference struck him dumb: he mistrusted his own ears; I saw the doubt in his looks; and twice repeated the same prayer.

"Heavens! what do I hear! Is it possible! Do not I mistake! The man you loved half an hour ago——"

"Is now the object of my hatred!"

"The transition is not natural! Wait till the first heat of your spite be over."——

"It is not spite, but a real contempt; that man I abhor!"

'And then I related what had passed.

"What!" exclaimed my father, "your affection for your lover cannot out-live the death of a squirrel? Pshaw! ridiculous! When you are cool, your love will return."

"It will not! Fancy had deceived my heart; this accident has dissipated the illusion: since I prefer my squirrel to Mr. Morley, I love him not!"

"Such an inconstancy at the minute you were going to be united! What will the world say?"

"What they please. Oh, dear father! sacrifice not your daughter to the opinion of a foolish world!"

"Who shall appease your mother? Her anger will be just."

"You yourself. Defend my cause: her love and her duty warrant me her forgiveness. Never did she oppose my father's pleasure."

"For a whim shall we break a match honourable in every respect?"

"Think of your daughter's happiness!"

"I would not make you unhappy; I am a father: but give some hours to reflection; you may repent."

"Never! never!"

'And I bedewed his hands with my tears.

'No longer did my father resist: the lawyers were sent away; and Mr. Morley, whom from that minute I constantly avoided, went to France, and forgot me. I thought I loved, Henrietta; yet the loss of a squirrel in one moment deadened my passion, and convinced me of my error. A squirrel only! How I would have laughed at those who would have maintained that the case might happen! You see, however, Henrietta, that they would have been right, and I absolutely wrong. We are not ourselves when we give way to passion: from this we receive a new understanding, with which we see what is not, and form judgments we should blush for, were we in cool blood.'

Some of the company she expected coming in, my mother whispered me—'Remember the squirrel!'

LETTER

LETTER II.

THAT anecdote of the squirrel, Susannah, made a strong impression on my mind.

'Is it possible that fancy should have such a power over our hearts as to command their feelings, and that from it our sensations should borrow their reality? I have heard men defend opinions evidently absurd; defend them so obstinately as to deserve oftener our contempt than our pity: like them, am not I an enthusiast, indulging an error from the fear of being enlightened? Illusions are so agreeable, who can wish for their loss? O that squirrel! that squirrel! I will put my affection for Mr. Romney to the test of dissipation and coquetry; leave every avenue to my heart open to infidelity. Lord Osenvor has true merit; to him I will listen: should it be only to please my mother, and take from her a real cause to complain and deny, I must make a few attempts to be free; her generosity will repay me. That squirrel, how strange!'

THE desire of being free, dear Susannah, was for five hours to me what the death of the squirrel had been to my mother: it took such possession of my head, as to cool the idea of Mr. Romney, and permit me to share, with a tolerable degree of vivacity, in the entertainment of our guests. I went even so far as to smile at the douceurs whispered me, and give them a song in praise of Liberty: I will tell you all; I was witty. After this demonstrative proof of indifference, my mother could not contain her joy.

'Never did I question your reason; though obscured, it's light was not extinguished.'

'Say my tenderness for you——'

'I am sensible of both. Henrietta, you are my daughter again.'

WHAT weak creatures we are! How readily we run from one extreme to another! How various the shades under which we may be seen! I do not wonder at the different opinions the world entertain of an individual: this man may be esteemed in one society, and despised in another; and that woman be mentioned for her indifference, whose heart burns with all the ardor of love. The fear I might be mistaken influenced me as an button does the courtier who bows from the minister he forms; it absolutely changed my nature: those who then saw me could have sworn to the insensibility of the sprightly, thoughtless Henrietta. The departure of the most gay part of the company I once used a relapse; not in conversation, no heart supported by the follies of youth and wit, drew back on the favourite object, to fill the trouble some vacuity it felt. Like the sun which never appears brighter than when it has been concealed behind a cloud, Mr. Romney's image revived in my heart: I saw him under the very features I wished him to wear; handsome, polishesent, and sincere.

'Oh! this is not the way to forget him,' sighed I: 'my attempt has added to his charms; my passion has increased; he is the deeper rooted in my heart!'

I wished for music to drown the secret whispering of love; their seduction was irresistible in the calm I was: I listened with the same complacency as I have viewed a picture of Correggio; every word, as every beauty, attracted my attention, and pleased my soul. I heard Mr. Romney, and I answered him as if he had been present: I forgot the squirrel, and thought of my lover.

LETTER III.

THE rest of the evening I supported alternately the different characters I loved; sometimes exerting an uncommon flow of gaiety, and now and then sinking into a reverie, or a soliloquy. This transition the indifferent could not perceive; but it did not escape my mother's discernment.

'Henrietta, beware of a reverie; it is a poison the more dangerous, that it is made of all the allurements of pleasure: from you I require only an impartial examination of two men of equal merit; wait till the presence of Lord Osenvor either confirms Mr. Romney's victory or defeat. If, in the mean time, you indulge the thought of your lover, you give him a confessed advantage over his rival:

'how can you value his worth, if you have no interest, or desire to know it?'

'I doubt Lord Osenvor's triumph!'

'That doubt makes too strongly against him; it is a prejudice you must not entertain, otherwise you would be both judge and party. I will have your passion undergo a fair trial, and be above the fear of sorrow. Let me be totally convinced that your love is not a chimera; but, that my belief be rational, you must not bribe your reason: let it coldly judge an determine. My consent I attach to your impartiality: deceive me not; I will be just.'

'You shall not complain; I will endeavour to obey.'

* *

This sudden turn in Mrs. Verman's disposition made me apprehensive for Mr. Romney.

'She would not so easily have promised her consent, had she not a certainty, either founded on her contempt of the passions, or her knowledge of my own character, that I shall change.'

Her confidence forced a mistrust of myself into my heart. At that time I did not think of the artful snare she had laid for me; I saw but reason and justice in her proceeding. By leaving me at full liberty to chuse, she weakened the force of the spirit of contradiction which naturally rises or falls in proportion to the more or less resistance it meets with: often is that spirit the whole reality of a passion; often does this, when no longer fed with obstacles, dwindle into indifference. Whether this motive, unknown to me, produced my new fears, I know not; I took them for the effects of the superiority which experience gave to my mother over me. If the former caused them, let me exclaim, again and again, 'What weak creatures we are!'

LETTER IV.

I Was just awoke from one of those enchanting dreams which nature, whilst reason is asleep, does sometimes favour our senses with, when Mrs. Moulton tiptoed to my bed.

'Will you forgive me?'

This she spoke with the stammering of a criminal.

'Forgive you!'

I was amazed, and searched for the truth in her look.

'What have you done, dear Madam, that you implore my forgiveness? You smile!'

'Some news from my lover,' thought I.

'Come, trifle no longer with my curiosity: what brought you here?'

'A cousin of mine; the ugliest fellow my eyes ever beheld: half of his face he left in the fields of Germany, and one arm in Canada. He has heard you was one of the prettiest women in England: and such is his esteem of beauty, that he comes from Dublin on purpose only to see you.'

'To see me! Fye, Mrs. Moulton!'

'Yes, Madam, to see you: and so prevailing his entreaties have been upon me, that I have promised to procure him the sight of your charms. He waits in the next closet, where I have locked him, for the moment you deign to appear. In favour of the motive, pity my poor cousin's impertinence: beauty is his foible; he would travel to Constantinople, were he certain to have a glance at the favourite Sultana.'

'This is downright madness: and you think I will receive his visit?'

'One minute only; he begs no more: will you grudge one minute when it can make a man happy?'

'A cousin of yours, you say?'

'Thus he calls himself. He asked the servants for his cousin Moulton, and was sent to me. He was so full of you, that I had not the heart to trouble him for the proofs of his being of my family.'

'There is some mystery in this: could it be Romney?' As I made this reflection, I slipped a gown on, and was soon dressed. Mrs. Moulton had such a grave face, that I did not know what to think.

I stepped to my dressing-room.

'Shall I, Madam, bring the man to you?'

'Do.'

And I leaned against the window.

* *

Mrs. Moulton came first.

'Pray, Madam, be not frightened at my cousin's horrible figure.'

And

And then entered the monster.

Although warned of his deformity, I shrunk three paces back with terror; and, turning my head, with my hand bid him to go.

'Oh, Henrietta!'

At the sound of the well-known voice, I wheeled about: it was my lover. The large black patch which covered his face he had taken off.

My surprize was great; my joy still greater.

'What! is it you?'

My heart betrayed itself in the few words I pronounced.

'Till I have heard you forgive, thus I will remain.'

And he fell at my feet.

'Do I want to say I do?'

He could not mistake my expression; he arose. How my heart panted! My hand lay trembling in his; the agitation of his spirits was equal to mine: for five minutes he could but sigh, but gaze; but sigh and gaze again. So tender a scene, Susannah! it was the first, it has been the last, my soul ever enjoyed!

LETTER V.

IN such a confusion Mr. Romney's unexpected sight had thrown my senses, that, being no longer able to support myself, I was nigh falling, when he received me in his arms, and placed me upon an elbow-chair. What a tenderness the languor of our spirits spreads over every motion, all over our countenances! It seems that those minutes belong particularly to nature, so still and silent are then both reason and modesty. My eyes wandered on my lover with an unspeakable delight; not once did the fear of being surprized by my mother intrude: of me my heart only felt; and it's feelings were those of love and pleasure. Like mine, Mr. Romney's eloquence consisted not in words; he talked the same language I did; without the help of our tongues we expressed and answered our mutual sentiments.

Mrs. Moulton, in bathing the temples of my head with Hungary water, disordered the handkerchief which already was too carelessly passed over my bosom. The sight of my breast animated Romney's eyes; I saw by the motions of his lips a desire to kiss it: then Virtue whispered—'Beware of thy 'senses, Henrietta! beware of thy lo-'ver's lips! They may diffuse so subtle 'a poison as—' Virtue stopped: I understood her. An air of dignity blending itself immediately with that of love, cooled the temptation in Mr. Romney's heart. His reservedness charmed me; the more so, as he could not doubt his pardon had he durst to offend. So respectful and disinterested a lover deserved a reward. I forgot the handkerchief, wished he would be less generous, and turned half my head: as Modesty instantly claimed her rights, my gratitude was a dead virtue; I must reward him with words; with a few—'I love you!—What I will say, I will 'feel: this will compensate for the kiss 'he has lost.'

* *

Mr. Romney had thrown himself on his knees before me, when Mrs. Moulton attempted to keep my spirits from sinking. There I suffered him; so pleased was he with his situation, it would have been a needless severity to deprive him of it. My hands I left in his: his discretion made me overlook favours I would not have granted, had he too visibly set a value upon them.

'This is, Henrietta, the very first 'day of real happiness I ever lived: the 'emotions you could not suppress, I 'have enjoyed to a pain. My Henri-'etta loves me; no other bliss am I de-'sirous of. Say you love me, that I 'may not think I dream. I am happy, 'happy so much beyond my expecta-'tions, that I still fear to be deluded. 'Say you love me!'

I hesitated, Susannah, to pronounce the mysterious words—'I love you!' not that I was afraid that my heart would belye my tongue; but education has given these words such a sense, such a character as to intimidate. Besides, does not the 'I love you,' like possession, deaden desire in a man? It takes from his soul the fiery activity of suspense. When certain of the bliss he panted after, like a hero in time of peace, he falls asleep under the laurels he has got.

How sad, on a sudden, that Mr. Romney, whose features had the moment before boasted his happiness, and expressed the delirium of pleasure! Men are great fools; so are we, Susannah! If, after what he had seen, he could not

'doubt my tenderness; after what I had
'written, my scruple was ridiculous. I
'pitied him, and pitied myself.
'Resume your spirits, Romney: I
'love you.'
'Is it then true?'
'Oh, too true!'
'That "too" is intolerable; it is
'torment to hear it: either it supposes
'a fault in me, or a fear in you not to
'be happy.'
'It does neither: I esteem you; there-
'fore entertain no apprehensions of
'that kind. But my mother, against
'you, favours another man. She in-
'sists on my submitting my passion to
'a fair trial; to judge between Lord
'Ofenvor and you; to be certain that
'I really love, before I give my hand.
'Her consent is the price of my compli-
'ance with her desires.'
'Did you tell Mrs. Vernan you
'loved me?'
'I did; and could not conquer her
'incredulity. By obeying her, I shall
'be yours: by disobeying, I may lose
'you.'
'I shudder at the thought of that
'trial; it is not a fair one, since my
'rival will be perpetually with you,
'and I am forbid your sight. Who
'will talk for me?'
'My heart, and your virtues.'

He would tell his gratitude: it was
too great, the words expired on his
lips. I rejoiced at my answer, so happy it made him.
'Dear, dear Henrietta!'
And he carried my hand to his heart.
'This beats only to you: it is ab-
'solutely yours. Never shall it re-
'ceive an impulse but of love: there
'no other passion will dispute your
'sway.'
'All your fears are now subsided;
'you will not wait with anxiety the
'event of the trial?'
And I amorously smiled upon him.
'How could I calmly hope for suc-
'cess, when my Henrietta is the prize
'of the contest? An earl for a rival!
'Henrietta, forgive if I fear; it is an
'involuntary offence; it proceeds from
'the greatness of your value, and my
'insignificancy. An earl!'
'You are a man: is there a nobler
'title? Have a care, Sir; humble as
'no, by thinking I may disdain vir-
'tue for the sake of a false grandeur,
'and search for happiness in the shewy
'scenes of life.'
'I have heard of Lord Ofenvor: his
'reputation is an honour to his rank;
'his virtues have added a new lustre to
'a name already deservedly famous by
'a long series of noble ancestors. He
'is not only an earl, but a man, such
'as you deign to call me: two so great
'advantages united in the same person
'—frown not, Henrietta—I have no
'fears; I am silent.'

LETTER VI.

THOUGH my lover said 'I have
'no fears,' a tear betrayed the
perplexity of his mind.
'Can you question my word? Is it
'thus you esteem me? Oh, Romney!
'be not unjust: your despondency is
'an insult I will not brook!'
'I love; you are the object: how
'should I be easy? Reflect on the
'power of my enemies. Lord Ofen-
'vor at a perpetual liberty to watch,
'and make the best of your sensibility;
'your mother perpetually speaking his
'praises, and abasing me.'
'Am not I your friend, Romney?
'What will opportunities and my re-
'spects avail them, when my heart is
'for you?'
'The ardent officiousness of an ami-
'able man, and the insinuating caref-
'ses of a mother, may weaken a paf-
'sion, and give it another turn. There
'are hours fatal to lovers: my happi-
'ness is so new!'
'Romney! Romney!'
'Be not angry at the tears I shed,
'at the fears I cannot dissemble. Had
'you only your beauty to boast, how-
'ever perfect, I might hope it would
'cause but admiration: your wit, your
'good sense, your talents, Henrietta,
'these are the qualities which call for-
'cibly for the love of the sensible, and
'fix you for ever in their hearts. Who
'could love, and not study how to
'please, to affect, to engage your af-
'fections?'
'But if they are already yours, can
'they be another's? Are our hearts so
'inconstant as to change and vary thus
'from feelings to feelings? I believe it
'not. I am more generous than you,
'Romney: it is my happiness to think
'you

'you shall be faithful, and never love
'any other woman than me.'

'This confirms my fears.'

'Why should I foresee what may
'never happen, when, at the moment
'I live, it may make me unhappy?'

'Your reason is too cool; you love
'me not.'

'Ungrateful man! Is this the re-
'ward of my affection for you?'

I could not stop the tears which his
suspicions forced from my eyes.

'My reason was too cool!' To keep
it so, what did not I suffer! How
many the sighs I had been obliged to
smother, the sobbings to suppress, the
sensations to disguise! 'You love me
'not!' His injustice was not to be
borne: it pierced my soul to be thought
false. I got up to fly from him; he
took hold of my apron, and with the
wild look of despair—

'Stay, Henrietta! stay, and forget
'your wrongs, or this minute my life
'will expiate for them. Life I scorn,
'if you forgive not. I have been guilty;
'but I love: I am not myself, Henri-
'etta! Say you pardon! my soul is
'upon the rack; relieve it from the
'agony it endures!'

'By you was I to be taught pain!
'Should it have been forced into my
'heart, after I had said—"I love you,
'" Romney!" A punishment for reward!
'From you did I deserve it?'

'Remember not my offence! it sinks
'me below the man and the lover: let
'one smile, charming Henrietta, an-
'nounce it is obliterated.'

'You never will mistrust me again?'
'No, never!'

I offered my cheek: why should I
dissemble with thee, Susannah? Upon
his lips I sealed his pardon.

'After this, Romney, be convinced
'you have nothing to fear.'

'Now,' said Mrs. Moulton, 'that
'you understand one another, you must
'for a few days take a farewel.'

'Why for a few days, Mrs. Moul-
'ton? Cannot I, to-morrow, under the
'same mask——

'To this day's calm a storm may
'succeed. I fear Mrs. Vernon's vigi-
'lant eye: your visit to me she will
'know, and not suspect you were the
'may ascribe to her daughter. You
'would be undone, were she to sur-
'prize you. A different garb must you
'assume when you come again: I will

'think of it.—Henrietta, another kiss,
'and send him away.'

'Both poison and balsam are in your
'words.'

A noise we heard in the library join-
ing to my dressing room, announcing
my mother, Mrs. Moulton pushed him
towards the door.

'But the kiss, the kiss!'
'Take it.'

He did, and went away.

LETTER VII.

'OSENVOR! thou hast no chance;
'or I know nothing of my
'heart!'

With this exclamation I sat down to
my toilet. The languor of my eyes
told too loud I had shed tears. I feared
her indifferent chit-chat.

'All is safe: he is gone,' whispered Mrs. Moulton.

'But these eyes will betray me.
'Though happy, I cannot give them
'their usual vivacity.'

'Well, cannot you say you have
'the head-ache?'

'I have it not.'

'Since truth offends, and falshood
'only can please, what other language
'can you speak? Would you, for an
'insignificant lye, break your mother's
'heart, and hazard your own happi-
'ness? That vice is oftener a virtue
'than we think.'

'No circumstance whatever can jus-
'tify it, Mrs. Moulton. It may be
'commendable to keep in our hearts
'a destructive truth, when there is no
'necessity of telling it; but if it is
'asked, and we are obliged to answer,
'it is base to conceal it. To what a
'contempt of myself my mother expo-
'ses me!'

'This moralizing, dear Madam,
'will not enliven your eyes; it is the
'worst remedy you could think of,
'the only one, I swear, that cannot
'cure. Come, cheer up your spirits,
'and behold the fine prospect that lies
'before you. A young, handsome,
'and sensible lover; days of content;
'nights of rapture! You smile; this
'smile is the very elixir which will
'brighten your looks: it has already
'operated: cast a glance at this glass;
'no need is there now to pretend an
'head-ache.'

'How

'How you talk!'
'As you feel, Henrietta. But hark! Mrs. Verman is coming.'

LETTER VIII.

'WELL, Henrietta, how does your heart?'
'Always the same, Madam.'
'There is an obstinacy in your distemper which requires an uncommon medicine: Lord Osenvor will find it, I hope.'
'From his hand I will receive it. I answer not for the effect.'
'It is Lord Osenvor's business to prepare it so that it may cure; yours is to take it.'
'However doubtful of his abilities, I will listen to the physician.'
'That is enough, Henrietta; I ask no more. His lordship will be here to-day or to-morrow. This letter I have just received from him. You may read it.'

'TO MRS. VERMAN.

'MADAM,

'I Have happily, and sooner than I expected, finished the business which called me here. It would seem as if Love, in my favour, had spoke to Fortune, so readily did some knaves at law forget their dishonesty, and make matters easy. Had not their deities come betwixt these jugglers and me, many months might I have been kept a victim to their insatiable avarice.

'No other affairs have I now but those of my passion for the lovely Henrietta: they are of the greatest moment; to them only will I attend. Free from the mortal cares which troubled my mind, I will give way to the feelings of my heart, and think of pleasing. This shall be my sole study: but, alas! I almost despair of succeeding. Though endowed with an exquisite sensibility, the charming Henrietta is gay and indifferent: never seriously would she listen to a declaration of love. She has such a contempt of my sex, as to distrust, if not to poison, the truest proofs of the inclination she inspires. She believes we are all false and immoral; that our language is rather the disgrace than the praise of beauty. Who can flatter himself to alter her opinion? The man she shall love may; who else, without her partiality, will not sigh, talk, hope in vain?

'Was friendship the sole sentiment I indulged, from my memory of her behaviour to me, I could think she favours me with hers: though delighted at her distinction of me, it is not love; and this only will satisfy my heart.

'Her looks, the preference she gave, told me I had no rivals: perhaps, had I durst to presume, would I have thought she really esteemed me; a compliment the more flattering, that it appeared to be the result of her reflections, that she was extremely cautious not to mistake in her judgment. She esteemed me; yet, when I spoke of love, I was immediately lost in the crowd of her admirers: then would she either answer my passion with wit, or with a severe look condemn it to silence. What a contradiction! Could I alternately deserve, and be unworthy of her esteem? She loved me not, Madam: this is the key to her conduct. Henrietta ever acted agreeably to reason; her delicacy I applaud. Sweet girl! would I could melt her soul with tenderness! Fortune has given me all that a mortal can wish for: but if she does not crown her favours with this bliss, they are of no value; of no avail to my happiness. I shall be miserable in the midst of riches and grandeur; nay, below the envy of the poor who can boast a woman's love. No true delights are there in life but those of natural desire; but those we procure and partake of: the other, not the heart, but the imagination, enjoys.

'Upon the promises you made me, Madam, when I left London, I totally depend; but, before I claim them, teach me how to please, how to deserve your daughter: her character you have formed; you must know your own work. Has her soul no generous foible which a lover can turn to his advantage? Miss Verman never could, without being unhappy, hear of another's distress: often did a tear betray her emotions. Will not her pity of my sufferings affect her
'still

'still more? That pity I have, Madam, I have seen several instances of: pity has many times dwindled into love. This thought has revived my hopes: I will order my chaise, and fly to London. I am, Madam, &c.
'OSENVOR.'

LETTER IX.

TWICE I had offered back to my mother Lord Osenvor's letter, and twice had she refused it, with—'No partiality, Henrietta; no partiality: keep your word.'

I read, and with as great a composure as I could naturally assume, returned it to her.

She laid her finger upon my heart.

'How does it beat now?'

'I feel yet no difference, Madam: that letter has only confirmed what I knew before; Lord Osenvor's merit, love, and delicacy. Would he were happy!'

'Is not this a concern—'

'Of gratitude only: that concern I cannot deny him.'

'Well, if this concern, so tenderly expressed, he cannot change into love, either you are not to be cured, or he shall have but himself to charge with the loss of your hand. Come, Henrietta, dissemble not: thy heart is big; thy eyes are crouded with tears; vent thy grief by throwing it off on thy mother's bosom.'

'Indeed, Madam, I have no grief to ease.'

'Henrietta! that tear; does it mean nothing?'

And with a kiss she swept that tear away.

I had not, Susannah, felt that tear trickling down my cheek. I sighed, and turned my face from my mother.

'Be not ashamed of that tear; it is an honour to your heart; such a sensibility is virtue itself: in it's favour I almost forget your love is for Romney; your pity for Osenvor. True generosity has a great power over me, Henrietta—deprive thee not of the pleasure of shedding a tear; it is the tribute of a noble soul to an unhappy man of merit.'

'I will own it; his letter has effected me: it is a torment to see miserable the man we esteem. Could he be contented with my friendship, no woman could be happier than I!'

'Judge of his feelings by your own, Henrietta.'

'He may have a greater command of himself: I am but a woman.'

'Like yours, his passions are inflexible; like yours, his reason is weak: no superiority has he to boast. We all are the children of the same nature.'

'Are there no degrees in sensibility? Do we all feel alike?'

'We do not. When our hearts are really enflamed, our affections are violent, lasting, and the same, in both sexes: when they proceed from fancy, they partake of it's nature, either ardent or weak; but they all, in general, end like a quick fire, which is soon destroyed by it's own activity. There are whims, tastes, caprices, and a hundred more insignificant inclinations, which, in their novelty, have sometimes the appearance of the passions; but passions they are not.'

'May not Lord Osenvor lay under a mistake?'

'Is it possible, Henrietta? But why should not you be deceived yourself?'

'Our cases are different.'

'How is that?'

'We seldom love when we have no hopes to move and engage the object we are smitten with: such hopes Lord Osenvor never could entertain; my indifference was too evident; his reason could not conceal it from him. But Mr. Romney's looks told me I might love: I had an incentive; his lordship had none.'

'Passion argues not thus, Henrietta; it has no need of encouragement: when the heart is affected, the head advises not. Could they listen to wisdom, would mankind be so often under the sway of folly? Such as labour under an imaginary distemper may reason themselves into health; but the sick—those who are really sick—on my word, dear girl, I wish Lord Osenvor was among the former.'

'That wish presages my happiness: from my mother's lips I have heard it.'

'Moderate thy joy, Henrietta; thou mayest not be among the sick—time will discover which of us is right;

'till then let me doubt, since I leave
'thee at liberty to think and feel at
'thy pleasure. Whether really in love,
'or unknowingly indifferent, forget
'not to consult thy glass for the dress
'which becomes thee the best. I will
'have you under arms against Lord
'Ofenvor's arrival, Henrietta; you
'must appear with all the seductions
'of art and beauty: not leave behind
'any charm that may captivate; you
'must strike both his heart and his
'fancy: the least neglect I will look
'upon as an attempt to disoblige; as
'an effect of your prepossession for
'Romney, and a violation of the agree-
'ment between us.'

'Would not this be a very ungene-
'rous proceeding, Madam? Why
'should I enflame the man I love
'not?'

'You may love him: you know not
'what changes the desire of pleasing
'makes in a heart.'

'Did not you bid me to be impar-
'tial?'

'I did.'

'When you expect such wondrous
'effects from the desire of pleasing,
'can you command I should make use
'of it?'

'That desire, Henrietta, will be the
'counterpoise of your taste for Rom-
'ney. By behaving thus, you shall
'keep him and Lord Ofenvor in a just
'balance.'

'You would not have me play the
'coquet?'

'As far as modesty allows; no far-
'ther, Henrietta.'

'As far as modesty allows! Did ever
'modesty allow to be false?'

'How came you, Henrietta, to act the
'reverse of what you thought, when
'you first saw Mr. Romney? At that
'time was not you false? Did not
'you use the arms of coquetry? Have
'you forgot the city-fop?'

'It was then an innocent weapon:
'I employed it not to hurt, but to
'strengthen, the passion of the man I
'thought I loved, to secure our mu-
'tual happiness.'

'You are grown of late, Henrietta,
'immensely refined in your notions!
'However, I beg you wou'd instantly
'compliment me with their d simission,
'and behave as a woman of sense: if
'you do, rely on my favour; if——'

My mother smothered the threaten-
ing; but I guessed it in the accent of
her voice.

'I have a few letters to write,' re-
sumed she, more calmly: 'get ready
'against three; we dine at the Countess
'Meyer's.'

LETTER X.

AFTER some observations on my
mother's behaviour, which my
respect for her did not permit me to
scrutinize, I rang for Mrs. Moulton.

'I want your opinion, dear Madam;
'give it to me with sincerity; flatter
'not. In me, see not your Henrietta,
'but a stranger; who, conscious of
'your wisdom, begs earnestly to be
'enlightened upon the situation of her
'heart.'

'Speak; I will be true.'

'My mother's incredulity, (I dare
'not call it obstinacy, or want of ten-
'derness) makes me sometimes mis-
'trust my own sensations: she is so
'positive that I love not; that Lord
'Ofenvor will invade in my heart the
'room which Mr. Romney occupies
'there; that she amazes my mind, and
'forces a doubt upon me. Spite of
'myself, I hesitate between her asser-
'tion and my feelings. Is it in her
'art or reason? Does she think as con-
'fidently as she talks? Am I really
'insensible, though with all the symp-
'toms of passion about me? From
'what you have seen and heard, you
'have certainly formed your judgment.
'What am I?'

Mrs. Moulton could not help laughing at the grave looks I had put on.

'How odd that question, Henrietta!
'Are you in earnest?'

'Indeed I am.'

And I sighed.

'Does not that sigh convince you
'that you love?'

'It may have another cause; answer
'me plainly.'

'Are you sure that you love?'

'Do you take me for a mad girl?'

'As well might you, Henrietta,
'doubt your existence, than to doubt
'of your love: the latter is as much
'proved as the former.'

'If it be so, why does my mother
'continue an unbeliever? Can she flat-
'ter herself to reason me into indiffe-
'rence?

'rence? Were the passions like opinions, she might hope to seduce me by the superiority of her wit: her eloquence could make me a convert; passion is not so easily overcome. Although I am so fond of pleasing her, she has not yet been able to persuade me; only a few doubts, which spring rather from my tenderness to her, than a real uncertainty, have perplexed my mind.'

'Send the impertinent intruders away, Henrietta: believe your own heart; it cannot deceive you.'

'How cruel to teaze me thus unmercifully! to teaze me to no purpose! for Mr. Romney shall be the man! What a contrast in Mrs. Verman's late conduct towards me! As her severity made against her, she grew complaisant and tender. How artfully, in our last conversation, she encouraged my pity for Lord Osenvor! She increased it by her insidious language; by the still more insidious share she affected to take in my concern for him. The tear I shed was her work; she laughed, I dare say, inwardly, at the foible she had created in my breast: though it was there before, it lay silent; she gave it life, and dissolved it into that tear. Lord Osenvor needed not her help to move me in his favour; I have a true sense of what he will suffer, and my soul unfeignedly partakes of it: I am unhappy to have inspired him with a passion I cannot return.'

'When he sees he cannot please, he will cease to love; a few months absence will compleat his cure. We do not desire long what it is not in our power to obtain: trust to time and your indifference; they will give him back the liberty he has lost. Were he so desperately enamoured as to brave their united efforts, well then——'

'What then, Mrs. Moulton?' She smiled.

'He may take a leap from the top of his castle: what a celebrity it would give to your charms!'

'Can you banter when I am so vexed? What is become of those feelings I always admired in you?'

'I do not lavish them upon imaginary distresses.'

'Are there any greater than to love in vain! How miserable I should be was Mr. Romney insensible!'

'I am sorry, for your sake, it is not fashionable to have two husbands; that would at once ease you of all your anxieties: you could take Mr. Romney for love, and his lordship out of pity.'

'Ridiculous!'

'Forgive the word, dear Henrietta; still more ridiculous it is to torment yourself, as you do, when you should enjoy your own happiness: you alone, of your sex, can be grave upon so trifling a subject. Had you twenty Lord Osenvors in your train, you should leave them all to their fate: you can love but one man; the rest, if their passions are real, may honour your wedding day by pistoling themselves before your window. Be not frightened; they will not do you that favour: for what I know, Lord Osenvor may the next day pay the usual compliments, and wish you joy.—Come, dear Henrietta, clear that brow, and let us talk of your lover.'

LETTER XI.

THERE was so much reason in Mrs. Moulton's humour, that I began to think it absurd to feel so warmly for the man I did not love.

'How shall I behave with him, Mrs. Moulton?'

'With your wonted generosity, Henrietta. Of your insensibility men cannot complain: you are not obliged to love, but to be just.'

'My mother bids me to receive him as a lover; to exert all my powers of pleasing.'

'And by this means to add to his wretchedness, and drive him to despair: that order is inhuman; virtue, not your mother, you must obey. By following the dictates of the former, you free your heart from remorse: a mother forfeits all her rights when she commands what it is a disgrace for her daughter to perform. Mr. Romney's attachment takes from you the necessity of being false: not one excuse does it leave you to palliate the debasement of your character. If

G 'you

'you have any respect for yourself, any esteem for Lord Osenvor, be true: though you should raise your mother's anger, you cannot be unhappy with the conviction of having acted agreeably to virtue.'

'These are the thoughts I ever indulged, Mrs. Moulton: but will Lord Osenvor believe me?'

'It is not natural he should: what is his incredulity to you?'

'A spring of new vexations it shall be: he—my mother—both will conspire against me! I shall be loaded with troubles!'

'Would not you despise the man who would thus repay your generosity? I know your spirits, Henrietta; they never will bear tamely with an undeserved persecution; the troubles you fear shall not affect you; your soul shall be entirely insensible of them. Remember you are an English woman, and not a slave: remember that, at your pleasure, you may be happy, and preserve the esteem of the world. Let Lord Osenvor sigh, talk of love, and rave himself into madness; let your mother threaten: your firmness will at last remove the former, and soften the latter; if not, take counsel of your heart, and bestow your hand on Mr. Romney.'

'His lordship may come every minute; it is time my irresolution should have an end: every thing is weighed; I am fixed; be the consequence what it will, your advice I will follow!'

LETTER XII.

YOU wonder not, Susannah, at the perpetual wavering of my mind; it's seeming contradictions your reason easily reconciles. Irresistible are the ebb and flow of the sensations carried from the heart to the head; in vain would we indulge this or that; we have no choice to make; an unexpected passion will intrude, and hurry us away from the thought we cherished. Thus, by the power of concurring circumstances, we have in the same hour two souls the reverse of each other.

The past made me apprehend for the future. However determined I was to execute the plan I had formed, should it not have the fate of the former? My mistakes had so closely followed one another, that three times I put that question to my reason; and as often did it answer a negative. Near two hours I employed to settle that point; and, as I had attentively considered it under every shape, I was overjoyed at the victory I got.

'Now,' exclaimed I, 'am I prepared to meet every obstacle with courage, and to act after my own heart! No longer shall I be blinded either by pity or filial love, and submit to the discretionary authority of a mother who would readily sacrifice my happiness to her ambition! Dissimulation I will not make use of; I will pride in my feelings, and Lord Osenvor shall be acquainted with them. If, far from respecting my passion, he has the baseness of availing himself of my mother's consent, then, as he shall be unworthy of me, contempt shall be my revenge.'

This reflection animated my resistance, and cleared my mind of the intolerable pain of uncertainty. I walked in my room with a lighter step: my breath was more free; it seemed as if it sprung from pleasure; and not with coquetry, but decency, I advised for my dress.

LETTER XIII.

WHEN my watch told three o'clock, I went down to my mother's: my air was easy; and in my eyes content prevailed.

'I do not like that gown, Miss; it is more rich than elegant; it thickens your shape; not these two months have you worn it! How came you to fancy it to-day?'

'I thought the colour modest; therefore very becoming.'

'Strange conceit! I wish you would speak your own language; this is a borrowed one.'

'From my mother I did not expect that reproof!'

'You did not expect that reproof!'

And she ridiculously mimicked the tone of my voice.—

'That tippet—good God! Why do not you put on a sattin handkerchief? it would not have been more inconsistent with your dress and the heat
'of

'of the day! I believe the girl is mad! Pray, take it off!'

'Would you have me be without one?'

'Why not? Is it not the fashion? Would it alarm your virtue?'

'It would indeed, Madam!'

'That virtue must not be very severe which a nothing could so easily endanger!'

I made a low curtsey, and stepped to the door. She arose with passion, and stopping me by the arm—

'Where are you going?'

'Into my room, till you deign to talk to your daughter!'

How she coloured, Susannah!

'Is this, Miss, an answer to a mother?'

I kept silent.

'Bold girl!'

And she returned to her chair. I made a motion to open the door.

'Stay!'

I obeyed.

'Whence your unusual pertness, Miss? Is Mr. Romney your master?'

'From you I learned it?'

This I did not say, Susannah; I smothered it on my lips.

'Lord! what a change that stupid passion has made in your looks and speech! I should not wonder to see you soon a Methodist! You will cut a most venerable figure among the brethren! Ah! ah! ah!—Fie, Henrietta! fie! Are not you ashamed of the impertinent form you appear under? What is become of that pride which at all times presided at your toilette, and made you display every charm? You did not then blush at a man's wanton eye: that eye you enjoyed with complacency, and always took it for praise.'

'Then, Madam, dressing not myself to please a particular object, I conformed to fashion, though inwardly I thought it wrong.'

'And so, Henrietta, the eager looks of an hundred men offended your modesty less than would have done those of the only one you would have been desirous to please? This is refined indeed!'

'I was hardly sensible of a coquetry which no man could boast to have caused: my heart, then innocent, would now be guilty; I will not make use of an art which my virtue disapproves.'

'Is not Mr. Romney, rather than virtue, the cause of so sudden a reform in your manners?'

'Both have determined me, Madam: since I love Mr. Romney, virtue forbids me to please another man.'

'That Romney you never shall marry!'

'Lord Osenvor shall never be my husband!'

No longer could Mrs. Verman contain her fury; she vented it in the most contemptible expressions: she forgot absolutely the mother, to shew me the tyrant.

'Too long have I,' said she with anger, 'too long have I indulged your obstinacy, and disguised my real sentiments, in hopes you would see and abjure your error. Till now I have employed only the language of persuasion; I wanted to convince, and not to command: since reason and my tenderness have no power over your conceited heart, since you are dead to the feelings of a daughter, and glory in your contempt of me, I will bid, and shall be obeyed. I will present Lord Osenvor to you; I will watch your looks and your motions; if they do not answer my expectations, for ever I renounce you; my fortune shall be my niece's; from this house you shall immediately depart: then, proud girl, offer a beggar to the arms of Romney; receive thy bread from his pity; debase thy soul by making it dependent of a man's generosity!'

And she flung herself into her closet.

LETTER XIV.

MRS. Verman's threatenings, Susannah, had upon my heart an effect she did not expect; they hardened it against her, and confirmed my resolutions.

'Since upon conditions only I have a mother, why should I, in her favour, make the sacrifice of myself? When she scorns her duty, and can think with indifference on exposing me to misery, is not the tie which bound us, her to love, and me to obey, effectually broken? It is lucky I had that 'tippet; it has helped me to an opportunity I could have long searched for and not met with: at another time I might not have had the same courage; and this, my love for Romney, and the shame of recanting, will make unalterable.'

I had just finished this internal soliloquy, when a servant came to let us know that the coach was at the door. I pointed to him the closet: thither he went.

'I have changed my mind,' exclaimed my mother; 'I will not go out. Tell Henrietta to retire to her room.'

With pleasure I heard that order. At that instant a loud rap exciting my curiosity, I stepped to the window. Lord Ofenvor! I flew; but, before I reached the stair-case, I met him on the top.

'Charming Henrietta!'

And he would have kissed my hand, had not I prevented him with an air of dignity and a severe look.

'Pray, my lord——'

'Heavens! what do I see?'

And he drew back, wondering at the coolness of my behaviour.

'My mother, my lord, is in her apartment!'

I curtsied; and to my own I went.

LETTER XV.

'NO more am I the timorous woman you thought me to be, Mrs. Moulton; I have behaved with the intrepidity of a hero!'

And I told her my scenes with Mrs. Verman and his lordship.

'Fortune has befriended you, Henrietta; make yourself worthy of her favour, by exerting all your reason in support of so happy a beginning. It is of no service if you relent: the most difficult of your part is over; the rest is easy to perform.'

'I will play it well; I have spirit enough to face either of them: my happiness is at stake; that inducement makes my success infallible. Fear not, Mrs. Moulton; far from decaying, my resolution will daily gather a new strength. Since in the two last encounters I got the victory over myself, since I could bravely act and speak, my heart is invincible, and my mind unchangeable.'

'Let me embrace you, Henrietta, in those noble sentiments I know you again; now you talk and feel as yourself.'

'Do not you think they are at this instant plotting against me? Lord Ofenvor has certainly told her the reception I gave him! How can she take it?'

'It is not easy to guess; the situation is extremely puzzling! I dare say Mrs. Verman will gild that reception so as to make it a matter of indifference; and that he has already forgot it. You may be sure she has not made him a confidante of your passion for Mr. Romney.'

'Fearful I should declare it myself, she may be before-hand, and give it as a foolish prepossession which will necessarily vanish with the absence of the man who caused it. That secret, disclosed by me, might discourage him: coming from her with the palliatives of wit and humour, it loses it's poison, and becomes a mere trifle.'

'She is too well acquainted with the character of a true lover to have ventured that discovery: however eloquent and artful Mrs. Verman, I doubt she could lull his fears asleep. A lover, Henrietta, is a being of a peculiar species, which knows no laws but his passion: had he no reason to be unhappy, he would immediately create twenty for thinking himself so.'

'Persuasion is on my mother's lips, Mrs. Moulton; and a lover credits easily what he has interest to believe.'

'The apprehension it is not, is ever the uppermost in his heart; but, I must own it, wit has great power: besides, passion has so contradictory shades; she may have spoke; he may have believed.'

A servant came: the dinner was upon table; they waited but for me. I had a mind to pretend an head-ache.

'They will think I fear; that I am still wavering.'

This reflection decided me.

'They will see, Mrs. Moulton, that I am steady.'

'If you come back conqueror, you may afterwards despise your enemy.'

LETTER

LETTER XVI.

MRS. Verman behaved with the pliantness of a politician, who at the call of self-interest adopts naturally a new voice and new manners. Though she did not treat me with her usual familiarity, she assumed enough not to let his lordship suspect a misunderstanding between us. As to him, he was at first sad, uncertain what looks he should put on, what language he should speak; but mistaking the gaiety I affected for a desire of pleasing, he grew chearful and very entertaining. A mysterious eye I surprized him casting upon my mother convinced me he knew my inclination; and the smile which succeeded it, his belief it was only an insignificant whim.

'You will not find it so, my lord.'

This answer I did not make, but wrote it legibly in my countenance.

Lest, from what I appeared to be, he should lay a claim to my heart and the liberty of complimenting me with his, I sunk gradually into a reserve which flattered him not, either with an opportunity, or the hope of success. I governed my spirits with such a dexterity so long as the servants staid, as to make their fall extremely natural when they were gone.

I could have spared myself the trouble of that gradation; for we were not five minutes alone before they were, seemingly, as dejected and stupid as myself.

How to open the conversation upon the topick they had at heart, they knew not. He begged, by his looks, she would begin; and her wink expressed—'Take courage, my lord. For shame!' and, 'You are a man!'

After what had passed before dinner, my mother feared to venture the first word, lest her pride should be humbled, and her authority over me put in question.

After a few such signs of encouragement, Lord Ofenvor opened his lips; but there his resolution died away.

It entered my head to tell him his thoughts and my own; my respect for Mrs. Verman opposed the fancy. I remained silent.

'My presence may intimidate him, He will talk if I go.'

This notion I easily guessed in my mother's sudden start from her chair, and careless departure from the room.

'Now I am going to be plagued,' said I to myself: 'since it must be so, it shall be, however, with pleasure. I will banter, lay Romney aside, and defend myself with wit.'

Lord Ofenvor's confusion continuing to disable his tongue—

'Why, surely, I may not hear of love if I chuse; let me find a subject, and keep it up. Why should not love itself be the subject.'

This idea, for it's boldness, pleased my reason. I considered it.

'It is the best I could think of.'

His lordship's more animated eyes announcing the end of his bashfulness, that soon he would dare to talk, I get up; and, after a turn or two in the room—

'I hope you are not sick, my lord.'

'Sick! not I, Madam.'

'Then you are in love; for I know no other cause which could make a man of your vivacity so pensive. I doubt not but the object of it is worthy so uncommon a reverie: my pride makes me think so, else it would be offended at your silence.'

'I love, charming Henrietta; I love, it is true: since you understood me so well, cannot you guess the woman?'

'Well, I am amazed that the gallant Lord Ofenvor has not already told me I am that woman. I excuse you, my lord: when men feel a real passion, they must necessarily lose their false civility: you was not so discreet as formerly; had I had then the imprudence to believe you, how miserable this minute I should be! But satisfy my curiosity; tell me the woman, I will not betray you.'

'Oh, Henrietta! can you mistake another for yourself?'

'Had you said this at first, it would have been very much a-propos; but now it is unseasonable. How could I be pleased with a compliment I have forced from you? Come, forget the courtier for the man of honour: use me as a friend; I hate a flatterer.'

'On my honour, I swear that I——'

'Stop, my lord; I am determined ne-

ver

'ver to believe the oath of any man whatever.'

'What a contempt of mankind!'

'It is a just one; you yourself, my lord, helped me to that resolution.'

'I! Heavens! how could I?'

'By talking to me of love, and not feeling it. Remember the daily declarations you made me during several months; reconcile them, if you can, with the coldness and levity of your carriage; every word was belied by your looks; at every visit you was guilty of the same falshood; the odious contrast at every visit offended my delicacy; since, at that time, you could sport with my judgment and your honour: but it matters not, you acted like the man of the world, and I knew his character; I laughed at your pretended passion, and esteemed you for your virtues.'

'You loved not, Henrietta; hence your error: you could not be the judge of my looks and feelings; had you been interested to believe them sincere, you would not have thus misconstrued them; they were the genuine effects of my love for you.'

'Go on, my lord. Love is a charming topick; like flattery, it does please the ear. You should have, however, thanked me for having rouzed you from your lethargy.'

'To hear you talk in this manner is still worse.'

'Do you intend this for a rehearsal of the part you are to perform before your mistress? Or do you act only to kill the minutes of a tedious tête-à-tête?'

Although the tone of my voice was not so expressive as my words, his lordship saw an insult in the jest. Indignation forced a colouring on his cheek.

'My lord,' said I to myself, 'has more pride than love; he will outlive his disappointment.'

An involuntary laughter accompanied the reflection I made.

'Am I so contemptible in your eye as not to be believed?'

Indeed, Susannah, from the indignation he could not suppress, I did not expect so moderate a question.

'Except upon matters of gallantry, my lord, I shall never mistrust your veracity.'

'What could induce me to say what I did not feel?'

'The want of diversion. Cards, plays, Ranelagh, leave sometimes a vacuity in your heart, which is always agreeably filled by a conversation with a young woman. You talk of love for the same reason that we women chatter about silks, ribbands, and hair-dress. The days must slip away, no matter how.'

'If you do not see a lover in his respect and passion, at what signs can you know him?'

'So well counterfeited, my lord, are now respect and passion, that hardly is there knowing the true from the false.'

'Yet you have——'

He paused. 'Now for Romney,' thought I. I was deceived. His lordship was too proud to do his rival the honour of mentioning his name.

'Does not, dear Henrietta, my character warrant my sincerity?'

'What has your character to do with the tittle-tattle you indulge? As well might you give it as a proof you ride, dance, or sing well. Tell me of a young, sprightly man of fashion, who does not glory in cheating a girl of her discretion? Who will not prostitute the most solemn oath in support of the most insignificant opinion? An oath is no better argument than a bett.'

'And you confound me with these men, Henrietta! Am I so low in your esteem?'

'Indeed, my lord, I esteem, sincerely esteem you: but why should I think you free from the foibles inherent to your education? Are they not looked upon as a prerogative of your rank? Men are tenacious of their rights; especially when they favour their passions.'

'I will say but one word; it will convince you: let us call your mother and a clergyman; this minute I am your husband.'

And he fell at my feet.

'On my word, my lord, you have excelled in this scene; you have brought it to a perfection Garrick only can boast; you have his looks, his motions, and his fall; I admire you: but now that the farce is over, let us play a more rational comedy; I will join with you in any part that discretion and modesty will suffer me to perform.'

'Insults

'Insults upon insults! Is this the language of Henrietta to the man who doats upon her!'

And he clasped my knees with both his hands.

'If you will not arise, my lord, and be yourself again, I will leave the room.'

'You will—'

And he looked wildly at me. His countenance frightened me. I pushed my chair back with violence; and, leaping to the chimney, rang the bell.

'Do you fear me, Miss?'

I did not answer. My mother entered the room.

'What's the matter? you rang as for an alarm!'

'My lord will explain it to you, Madam.'

'Cursed love!'

This was Lord Osenvor's.

I left them together.

LETTER XVII.

DID not I, Susannah, come off handsomely from that unpleasing interview? I must own it, Lord Osenvor gave me a superiority which I might not have boasted, had he been tender and passionate; but his flights from love to indignation kept my spirits to their height. In the same circumstance, Romney would have affected my soul; his pride would have been silent in a scene consecrated to love.

A nobleman has a natural haughtiness, impatient of resistance. Uncontrouled in his desires, the provoking facility he has of satisfying them makes him a child, from the man he was, when he meets with an unexpected opposition. With other men, the reigning passion commands; with him it is subservient to twenty, whose foolish delicacy a nothing will alarm and irritate.

'He loves himself more than me; therefore he will be ungenerous.'

This conclusion, like me, Susannah, you would have drawn. I prepared myself against the hurricane I foresaw I should be exposed to; and the following letter from Lady Bennet confirmed my hopes I should not suffer by it.

※ ※

'TO MISS HENRIETTA VERMAN.

'DEAR HENRIETTA,

'MY nephew has told me his happiness; he feels it as he ought: no greater can fall to the share of a man. Thanks from me you do not expect; they would not repay your favours. I have but that nephew; you only I wished for my niece: the day, when your hands are united, I will think the most fortunate of my life. From my knowledge of your mother's character, I am certain you must not rely on her fortune; it is lost to you; this assurance increases our joy as you shall be fully convinced of Romney's disinterested love, and my real affection for you. Make not yourself uneasy through a false delicacy; it would be an insult upon us; your tenderness, and not gratitude, we want.

'Lord Osenvor, Mrs. Verman thought of for your husband: however dangerous such a rival, I forgave not my nephew his fears. After you had said—"I love you, Romney," he could no more doubt you constancy than your inclination.

"These words from her lips," have I told him, "were a security it was a prophaneness to question."

'He cast his eyes down, was ashamed of himself, and sighed—

"Never will I be guilty again."

'In Romney, dear Henrietta, you will find real probity, and a sincere love for the duties prescribed by religion and law. Though with four thousand a year of his own, and the absolute command of my purse, not once yet has he deserved the censure of men; not once slandered virtue and patronized vice. He partakes of all fashionable diversions as a man, and not with the enthusiasm of a dissolute youth. His judgment he formed by travelling; not like our great men, either drunk or asleep, or careless of instruction; but studying with attention and impartiality the genius and manners of the nations he visited. Did I know, dear Henrietta, a fault in his character which could cause one hour of trouble in your whole life, I should think it incumbent upon me to warn you of it; his happiness

'I would

'I would disregard, to save you from sorrow. But I discover none capable of affecting your peace, and stopping the course of your felicity; on my word, I know none.

'If Lord Osenvor's assiduity is troublesome, think of the remedy. Our arms are open to you. My dear, lovely Henrietta, Adieu.

'M. BENNET.'

'P. S. I love you. These words only does my cruel aunt permit me to write.

'ROMNEY.'

LETTER XVIII.

'HERE is a safe retreat against the storm, Mrs. Moulton.'

'Would not it be prudent to shelter into it before it comes?'

'What a coward you are!'

'I should not like to encounter a danger I might avoid: there may be heroism in braving it.'

'There is none, Mrs. Moulton: it is a false glory which the brave disdain.'

'So you are determined——'

'To wait till the storm begins.'

'To wait till the storm begins! It will be high time, then, indeed, to think of a refuge.'

'I may be in no need of it. Many incidents may dissipate it before I am unable to endure it. I have told it you, Lord Osenvor loves me not.'

'You are pleased to believe so. It is impossible; he must love your person. Such a shape! Henrietta, he loves you.'

I smiled, and put my hand on her lips.

'His pride is too quick to suffer long my indifference. Two such other visits, and my slave is gone: no longer will he grace my train.'

'Your gaiety is a delight to me, charming Henrietta! But if, out of revenge, he would continue to court and abuse basely of your mother's approbation——'

'That is the storm, Mrs. Moulton, I am afraid of. He has behaved so as to make me apprehensive of his being indelicate and ungenerous. This has been the first time he gave me one reason to repent of my esteem for him. Young men of his rank have a fierceness in their actions, an impetuosity in their desires: my modesty took the alarm, and was put to a blush. Had I not arose from my chair, I should have been forced in his arms. "Do you fear me, Miss?" asked he. That question made me hate my mother, who had exposed me to hear it. How bold that man! Such proceedings love may excuse, but justifies not!'

'Such a beginning threatens——'

'He has real honour, Mrs. Moulton; this may silence his passion.'

'It is a perhaps.'

'I will indulge it till future events convince me I am wrong.'

'What a heart! What a treasure for for the man you love! Happy, thrice happy Mr. Romney!'

'I wish I could still add to my feelings, so deserving I think him of them: to please and be esteemed by the man we marry, must be an inexhaustible spring of delights; none but these I would be ambitious to enjoy. It is oftener our fault, Mrs. Moulton, than that of an husband, if we are not loved and happy. Each sex hath it's virtues: man's opinion; ours, decency sways. If we invade their privileges we must necessarily sink into disgrace and contempt.'

'Reason is sometimes for women, Henrietta.'

'Virtue is always against them. Reason is no apology for foibles which virtue condemns.'

'I believe his lordship is going; I hear the noise of a coach.'

And she peeped through the window.

'It is he! Mrs. Verman with him! there is a conspiracy.'

'If he is my enemy, he will be an open and generous one: from him I fear no deceit; he will dare whatever he resolves.'

'I have a mind to send after them for intelligence.'

'Ridiculous! Step down till I call. I will retire into my own heart, and see what I must do.'

LETTER XIX.

FROM their going out together what could I infer? Nothing. What else are conjectures? No new
'light

light did they throw in my mind upon their conduct; no new poignancy did they give to my fear of them.

'I must be forced to Lady Bennet's, and not leave my mother before she herself has forsaken me. Romney would love me less, did I, without an evident necessity, accept the asylum he offers: when a daughter takes such a step, she should be certain that none against her will or can take her mother's part.'

The censure of the world, however unjust, Susannah, I always feared. I always thought it a disgrace not to be esteemed by all; the secret whisper of slander, what virtuous woman can bear? Had I ever fancied myself the object of one, I would have died with shame, or never durst to appear again.

* * *

The rest of the evening I shared between love and musick: Mrs. Moulton and my harpsichord made it unfelt glide away; not one intruding thought on the possibility of a disappointment. I talked of Romney, sung, played, was totally lost in the sense of my happiness.

* * *

Do we feel a pleasure, pain is at hand ready to succeed it; without their mixture we should be unhappy. A few days of sickness give every sense a new life: our desires are animated with a fire unknown before; nature itself appears under a more enchanting form; it seems we enjoy our existence but from that day we have recovered. Susannah, this philosophy I needed the next day, when my courage was ready to sink under an unforeseen event.

LETTER XX.

IT was hardly five o'clock in the morning when I awoke at the sudden uncommon noise of horses, carriage, and servants, at the door. 'What does this mean?' I was not long left in suspense. My mother presented herself as I was slipping a gown on.

'Dress yourself immediately, Miss; you must this minute set off for the country; there you shall learn to be dutiful and obedient; the horrors of a wilderness will soon abate your obstinacy, and cool your fantastical passion; they will help you to the true knowledge of yourself.'

Her tone of command, added to her sneers, destroyed the terror which her speech had struck me with.

'This method, Madam, will not succeed.'

'I will try it, however.'

'Who has answered for my compliance?'

'My own authority, Miss.'

'As a mother you have, as a tyrant you have none. I am free, not a slave.'

'You have, of late, Miss, immensely improved the practice of your duty.'

'Have not you your own to fulfil, Madam? Is it your duty to make your daughter miserable, to force my inclinations, when I love a man whom, was you a mother, you would delight to give me for a husband? He is not an earl! Should this be an objection if you loved me? Do not his virtues compensate for the want of a title?'

The truths I spoke were too sensible not to throw Mrs. Verman into confusion; she had hardly the spirit to affect an air of indignation. My reproofs were keen, but deserved, and my tongue gave them their own expression. Such a firmness she had not thought of.

'Will you give me your word never to marry that man without my consent?'

'It may never be obtained: my gratitude for his generosity forbids me to promise.'

'And so you will marry him?'

'Never will I another.'

She walked pensive, irresolute, and animating herself to a bold stroke of despotism.

'The world will never hesitate between you and me: my age and experience secure me the general approbation for whatever measures I may adopt to restore an infatuated daughter to the reason she has lost. All will think I act from the consciousness I am doing right; your complaints will not avail you. I am a mother; that character mankind reveres.'

'When that character is not supported, the respect it inspires dwindles soon—'

I durst not proceed, Susannah.

'Into contempt. Is not this the word you have smothered, Miss? From 'you this usage! What! already lost to decency, as well as to filial love!'

'Look into your heart, Madam, and dare to judge me: if my expressions offend, your severity is the cause. In your breast pride has invaded the rights of nature. You are a woman, and not my mother; it is the former I speak with.'

I was too affected; I could suppress neither sobbings nor tears.

Shame, art, or a remain of tenderness, altered, in a minute, Mrs. Verman's looks and accent. She drew near me; and, inclining upon the bed—

'Am I to be hated by Henrietta, when I sincerely intend her happiness?'

I threw both my arms round her neck.

'Why have not you always these looks, this accent? they are persuasion itself. I am loth to mistrust you, when thus you talk, when thus you look upon me. You intend my happiness; yet will mistake the man, the only man who can procure it me.'

'Was your passion, Henrietta, the work of time, I would not doubt it's reality. But Romney twice only you have seen! Who can charge my incredulity with malice or folly?'

'Am I not the best judge of my own affections? Believe me, no need is there of a trial; spare your heart the share it must necessarily take in my sufferings; let me no more lose my mother. You feigned an anger you had not, an indifference you would abhor to feel: your dissimulation nature has betrayed.'

'You might be a countess, Henrietta! Have you no ambition?'

'It is centered, dear Madam, in Mrs. Romney's name. I know no greater, since none can make me so happy.'

'I cannot reflect, without pain, on your loss of a rank you was born and brought up to deserve, and fill with dignity. Henrietta, it requires more virtue than I have, to bear patiently with it. Why do not you feel as I taught you to think? I love you; but I love myself: too cruel is the sacrifice you exact from me. I have told you my foible; indulge it with a few attempts against your inclinations for Romney: retire into the country for a few days; there, for a few days, suffer Lord Ofenvor's assiduity; deny him no opportunities to please; clear your mind of any prejudice he may have thoughtlessly prepossessed it in his disfavour.'

'These few days will be days of vexation and agony. I cannot love him.'

'If, then, you do not, no longer will I insist upon your obeying me.'

'What place have you fixed for my exile?'

'Felton-Lodge in Sussex, at my sister's.'

'Will Mrs. Moulton follow me?' She paused. 'She shall, Henrietta.'

I did not like her hesitation—'Is she still talking deceit? Is it not imprudent to go? A few days only the talks; and Mrs. Moulton will be with me: in her company, what have I to apprehend? However violent the measures they intend to carry, they cannot force a "Yes" from my lips. I will go.'

'Though conscious of the inutility of this journey, Madam, I will undertake it to please you.'

Her eyes brightened with joy, and she pressed me tenderly to her bosom. The excess of her joy was not natural. 'This is all imposture,' sighed I. 'Some design they have premeditated against me: when I am once in their power, it may not be easy, nay perhaps it will be impossible, to steal away from them.'

This reflection made me sad, diffident. I was tempted to go from the promise I had just made. I looked fixedly at my mother: she was as calm as innocence.

'Come, Henrietta, the morning is beautiful; let us not lose it. I will ride with you to Felton-Lodge.'

'Do not you purpose to stay there, Madam?'

'No, dear girl; but every day you shall hear from me.'

New fears, Susannah, crouded into my head. 'Would she smile upon me with mischief in her heart? A mother!' I durst not give way to suspicion. I dressed; Mrs. Moulton was called; and away we drove.

LETTER

LETTER XXI.

POOR Mrs. Moulton! so hastily had she been hurried to the coach, that she had neither time to put a single question, nor to enquire into my looks, for the cause of so sudden, unthought-of a journey. Her uneasiness I immediately removed, by telling her, with a smile, the place we were going to.

Mrs. Verman's chearfulness kept me from feeling too sensibly, that every mile we rode encreased my distance from Mr. Romney.

'This short absence will heighten
' our happiness: we shall see then one
' another with a greater pleasure; a
' real bliss will result from this imagi-
' nary evil.'

With such reflections I arrived at Felton Lodge, with a tolerable degree of vivacity and content.

Mrs. Spencer received us with the smiles and half courtesies of a woman proud of her riches, and of my mother's being in need of them. This assurance spread an offensive coldness upon her countenance. 'I am at last courted by
' a sister still prouder than myself.' As Mrs. Verman seemed not to understand this meaning of her features, I whispered it to her: she had too much wit either to hear or answer me. My aunt's looks at me agreed perfectly with her behaviour to my mother. As she kept constantly in the country, and we lived in London, three years had elapsed since she saw me; I was therefore quite a new thing exposed to her view. 'Well
' enough; rather too impertinent and
' affected; a spoiled child, to whom, I
' must, and will, teach better manners.'

Had Mrs. Spencer spoke these words, she could not have expressed them better.

' If my mother will overlook this
' woman's impertinence, I shall not.'

And advancing to her with the utmost politeness—

' I thank you, dear Madam, for your
' good opinion, and the instructions
' you lovingly purpose to give me.'

' What does the girl mean? Did I
' speak to her?'

' Your tongue has not; but these eyes
' have, Madam.'

And, turning gravely to Mrs. Verman—

' I believe our visit is disagreeable:
' you would not surely have me stay
' where I am not welcome.'

Mrs. Spencer burst into a laughter.

' Come here, you fancy Harriot;
' come here, I say; I will kiss you for
' your seasonable rebuke. What! you
' have pride enough to resent my con-
' duct; and you do not blush at the
' preference you give to Romney over
' Lord Osenvor? A girl of your sense
' to commit such a blunder! You may
' bring a coronet into our family, and
' will thus unmercifully beggar us of
' it. You shall not, on my word. I
' will make you wise, I warrant you.—
' Sister, I will take care of this charge.'

I thought I perceived, in the tone of her voice, a satire levelled at Mrs. Verman, and that she would not be my enemy.

' I have not offended! How trans-
' porting the thought!'

' I was pleased, Henrietta, and not
' offended. Had you tamely suffered
' my contempt, I would have hated
' you. I love a girl of spirits: there is
' a glory in taming them. Shake not
' your head; I will succeed. My con-
' stancy in teazing and plaguing you
' out of your inclination, I will force
' you to admire. You shall ackno w-
' ledge me your conqueror. But I for-
' get, you must have got an excellent
' appetite, let us dine: after that we
' will enter the lists, and fight bravely
' for victory.'

LETTER XXII.

MRS. Spencer's charming sprightliness diffused itself into my heart: I humoured her fancy; and was as gay and thoughtless as if I had been perfectly happy.

' You see, sister, my niece and I are
' already upon friendly terms: we will
' soon understand one another; I dare
' say we shall not differ.—What think
' you, Harriot?'

' It is my opinion, Madam.'

Indeed, Susannah, from a wink she had cast at me, I was convinced she would favour my passion; and I was not deceived.

' Envy me not my conquest, sister,
' since the benefit shall be wholly
' yours.'

' Let us be generous enemies—Here
' is to poor Romney.—Come, sister'

'With

'With all my heart.'

We all drank to poor Romney.

'Why did not Lord Ofenvor wait there upon my lovely girl? He a lover!'

'He could not poffibly. He will be here this evening, or to-morrow.

'Is he handfome, Harriot?'

I was deaf.

'And Romney?'

'Very much fo.'

'He is not an earl. This title has a beauty which beats all Romney's charms to nothing: that bofom fhould not be prophaned but by a duke. Your Grace here, Your Grace there; it feduces one's reafon to think of Your Grace. Were I you, Harriot, I would force the proudeft of the nobility to lay at my feet: to marry the man you love is fo ftupid a refolution as not to enter a rational head; you fhall be a perfect flave. Inftead of commanding, you will be in a perpetual trembling not to obey quickly enough; all your paffions will center in that of making him happy. Fie, Henrietta! for one man bid adieu to pleafures, diffipation, the flattering gaze of a world of adorers; to fink all at once in the wife! I have no patience. Silence; I know your anfwer. I deteft preaching after a good dinner; it troubles one's digeftion: no more of thofe men for to-day; let us enjoy the remains of it.'

As we were ftepping to a parlour next the garden, fhe gave me a gentle tap on the fhoulder, and whifpered—'Fear not.' I carried her hand to my lips, and printed upon it a kifs of gratitude.

※

Lord Ofenvor did not come. Mrs. Verman having fixed her departure for the next morning, we retired early to our apartment,

'You know my wifhes, Henrietta: I will fay no more. To-morrow I will be gone before you are up. Write to me.'

I begged a motherly embrace.

'Never doubt my tendernefs. This is the firft time I have parted from you: it pierces my heart.'

She ftrained me to her bofom.

'Leave me, Henrietta! Go to reft: I feared this inftant! I—leave me!'

And fhe faintly ftruggled to get free from my arms.

'Dear mother!

'You love me. I am confcious you do.'

She put her handkerchief up to her eye.

'Muft I fee that real concern, and yet difpleafe my mother! How hard my fate! Take me back with you to London.'

'I am too weak, Henrietta, to be juft either to you or myfelf. From what it coft me to leave you behind, I fhall not long be without you: your abfence, I fear, will plead too well for you. Go; I infift upon it.

I refpected her grief, and went to my room.

LETTER XXIII.

AS I was neither fatigued nor inclined to fleep, I fat up two hours with Mrs. Moulten. From Mrs. Spencer's 'fear not,' we concluded I fhould be happy.

'How grieved Mr. Romney, when he hears you have thus precipitately left the town; when nobody can tell him where you are gone! From his love judge his defpair. He will fuffer beyond your imagination.'

'He will love me the more when he finds me. This night a letter cannot be fent. To-morrow, my aunt—from her I have all to hope: fhe will be propitious to me. Romney fhall know I am here. My mother dreamed not I fhould find a protector in Mrs. Spencer; nor did her reception at firft flatter me with it. I am impatient to fee her. There is no deceit in her fmiles. The "fear not," her heart fpoke. Lord Ofenvor will lofe the day.'

※

Mrs. Spencer, Sufannah, longed for a converfation as much as I did. She thought fhe could not too foon difpel my apprehenfions, and make me happy.

An hour after my mother was gone, fhe tript up to my room.

'Scold me not, Henrietta; the lofs of your fleep I will compenfate.'

'I needed not that affurance to believe you; from your lips I cannot hear but what will delight my heart. You talked and behaved in fuch a manner yefterday as to confirm my
'hopes.

'hopes. I enjoyed that day which I dreaded would be marked with sorrow. Here have I met with a friend instead of a persecutor.'

I threw my arms round her waist.

'You have, Henrietta; you have indeed.'

And she embraced me with an uncommon fondness.

'My sister sent me an express the night before, and begged I would receive you for some weeks, and suffer, and support with all my interest, the visits and pretensions of Lord Osenvor. She treated your passion for Mr. Romney of a childish whim, and expatiated upon the advantages resulting to the whole family from a marriage between his lordship and you. So brilliant an establishment, I own, Henrietta, prejudiced me against you. I fell blindly into her opinion, and prepared my heart to oppose your tears, and destroy an inclination I fancied a real disgrace. You came: at your sight I was moved. I mistrusted that heart; it was not armed against the power of beauty, and the enchanting allurements of the happiest physiognomy I ever beheld. Your shape, your motions, the tone of your voice, had a charm I could not resist. "I cannot hate her," said I to myself; though, in the mean time, to please your mother, I threw at you the looks of indifference and contempt. Your sensibility, which took the alarm, and returned upon me the contempt you deserved not, parted instantly from me the true from the false woman. It made me your friend. I prided in a niece who durst to act with magnanimity, and brave openly her enemy. Your behaviour convinced me of the sincerity of your passion. I scorn to make unhappy the girl I can boast to esteem. Although Romney be not Lord Osenvor, since you love him, he is the man I will favour. Thank me not, Henrietta; words would not express half the gratitude which enlivens your countenance: this only does repay my tenderness for you. Dress yourself; and after breakfast we will lay our wise heads together, and fix the fate of Lord Osenvor.'

'How shall I requite such goodness!'

She would not hear, but shut her ears with both her hands, and left me.

LETTER XXIV.

AT breakfast Mrs. Spencer called all her servants to the hall; and, presenting them to me, ordered them to obey whatever I should command.

'You are not my slave, Henrietta, but your own mistress. A young woman of your judgment and spirit from me shall receive no law.'

'Would I were worthy of the favours you bestow upon me!'

'This wish acquits you. By acting as I do I gratify a favourite passion, Henrietta. I am proud to shew I know your worth: so I please myself, you owe me no obligation. Now that we are alone, let us settle how we must behave with his lordship. From what my sister has told me of his excellent qualities, I think we should coax him into generosity, and seem to rely upon him alone for your happiness. This conduct must operate upon a noble heart. In giving you up to his rival he will forget the sacrifice for the glory of having made it. Have you a better advice to offer?'

'Indeed I have none. Yours agrees so perfectly with my esteem of him, that I hardly doubt it's success.'

'Well, we will follow it. Have we any other concern to unravel? You sigh, Henrietta.'

'Romney knows not what is become of me. What anxiety he must be in!'

'It is cruel in your mother to have overlooked the torments he should suffer; they are not to be borne by a lover. It was inhuman: let us find an antidote to that poison.'

I was stupid, Susannah, from the want of shewing my gratitude; not a word of that would she listen to: it made me almost faint.

'Write to Romney, Henrietta: tell him you are safe; but hide from him the place you live in. Prudence requires that the two rivals should not meet. Go, lose no time; forget not to write lovingly.'

And she smiled.

LETTER

LETTER XXV.

TOO pleasing was the order not to be instantly complied with. I stepped into her closet, sat down, and wrote what my heart dictated.

TO CHARLES ROMNEY, ESQ.

'THOUGH never so great the pains you endure from my absence, they are my own, dear Romney. My departure was so sudden, so unexpected, that I had it not in my power to warn you of it. I am safe at a relation's, who doats upon me. She was to be my tyrant; such were my mother's expectations: she has turned a friend to me, to you, Romney. You she loves, and wishes for my husband; doubt not this, and I will reward your credulity. My heart is thine; thou hast nothing to fear: the few days I am led to stay, think of me. Increase thy love, by calling to thy mind the few virtues thou thinkest I possess. Fancy I am in thy company, listening and answering thy raptures. I love thee, Romney. Tell Lady Benn, I love her. Believe both, your faithful

'HENRIETTA VERMAN.'

I presented the letter to Mrs. Spencer, that she might read it.

'Have no ceremony, Henrietta; seal it. One of my people will carry it. The slowness of publick couriers would answer ill the impatience of thy heart. Romney shall have this letter before dinner, and not know whence it came. Possibly we may have an answer at night.'

Had you been me, Susannah, you would have admired the turn of your fortune, loved your aunt, and been silent.

Part of the morning we walked and read away. No troublesome thought pressing upon my mind, I gave way to my natural gaiety, and expected, without fear, Lord Ossory's arrival. We saw him at one o'clock in the avenue, followed by the house, mounted on his charger, attended by three servants in close [...]

'I was about to forewarn you, Henrietta, you be the character of that chariot. Had you his love, it would

'stun your reason. Pride is always heard when we are indifferent. Humble him not, by hinting he is the cause of your retreat: he will repay your discretion with generosity.'

The chariot then entering the yard, we went down to receive his lordship. From Mrs. Spencer he had a very hearty welcome, from me a polite—'I hope you are very well, my lord.' He took my hand, and, for this time, I suffered him to kiss it. The tedious formality of an indispensible ceremony over, we began to talk with the freedom of friendship.

Whether out of compliment to my aunt, or merely to please himself, he would take a view of the house; but such a long time he employed in her closet of natural curiosities, as to make me conclude his love was not of the fine nature as mine. Romney would not have preferred the examination of a shell, or a medal, to the pleasure of conversing with me; this would have been the only way he would have felt and gratified. By gradual imperceptible steps I withdrew to the library, and left him with Mrs. Spencer. For half an hour more he continued in that closet, whilst I amused myself with Clarissa.

His lordship was in rapture at what he had seen. 'How prodigiously rich and well chosen that collection!' Till now he had boasted his own; for the future, never would he mention it. Compared to Mrs. Spencer's, it was a poor one indeed. How came she by such a rare variety?

'This man loves you not,' whispered my aunt; 'I believe he would barter you for the tenth part of my collection.'

I burst into laughter.

'Will you propose the bargain?'

'No, no. I should suffer by it, since he cannot have you.'

His lordship walked up and down the library, admiring the fine order in which the books stood, and now and then a bust attracted his attention, and forced an eulogium.

'In this house, dear Henrietta, it is impossible you should regret the diversions of London.'

'My aunt's friendship makes me insensible to their loss.'

'Does not my presence contribute a
'little

'little to that indifference? Am I for nothing in that tranquillity of mind you appear to enjoy? If I am mistaken, out of pity, dissemble; undeceive me not—let me cherish the flattering error; next to life, I would hate to lose it.'

'He loves his life better, however,' said I to myself: 'my frowns will not carry him to the grave; I am glad of it.'

'The company of an amiable man, my lord, is always desirable. I know but one I prefer to your lordship's.'

'It is kind in you; but there is still too much: were I that one, I would be the happiest of mankind. Let me be the first in your heart.'

'Though you deserve the first, my lord, you must rest contented with the second place; it is not in my power to give it to you: let us be friends, since you cannot be my lover; the greatness of your soul will make your victory easy; you will not make me miserable, when you can insure my happiness. No, Lord Ossenvor will not have Henrietta unhappy.'

'It would tear my heart to see you really so. I the cause, Henrietta! Pray, spare me: talk not thus.'

'I knew your lordship's magnanimity; your virtues were my warrant. I was certain you loved me for myself; that your soul would disdain to force my inclination, and punish me for a fault I was not guilty of.'

I took his hand affectionately into mine.

'Now you are yourself, my friend, my benefactor. I am happy,'

And I kissed the hand I held.

'Heavens, Henrietta! what are you doing? What have I said that deserves such thanks? I am your friend, it is true: but, oh! what a conflict is this!'

And he led my hand to his heart.

'Courage, my lord; give way to your generosity: pity your Henrietta.

And I involuntary fell at his feet, with tears in my eyes, and pantings in my bosom. I would have spoke; the words dwindled into sobbings.

'Arise, thou virtuous girl! Arise, lovely Henrietta! You affect me too much: let me breathe. At my feet!— Fortunate Romney! Unhappy me!—

'Arise! I am ready to sink! I was not prepared for this encounter: my sensibility you have struck, and commanded! Fear me not, Henrietta!— Mrs. Spencer, help me against her tears; they unman me.'

'They have rather made a man of you, my lord; they have restored you to your own dignity, obscured by an unlucky passion. Never have you appeared to a greater advantage. I love and revere you for her esteem of you. I admire your lordship for the triumph you have obtained over yourself.'

'Compliment me not upon a doubtful victory; it is not yet compleat: Henrietta cannot be so easily erased from my heart. Hide these tears from me, or I am undone; I have no strength against them. Too many enemies have I to meet with: her sorrow—You, Mrs. Spencer, whom I thought for me—'

'I have a tender soul, my lord; it dissolved into pity at her sight. I conquered my pride. As you was the man destined for my niece, that pride was very great; yet I conquered it: like me, my lord, you will conquer your passion. Look on Henrietta; think of the happiness you may procure her. Are not you happy to have it in your power? Can man boast a greater?'

He sighed; and, on a sudden, straining me to his bosom—

'Though my passion be extremely fierce, I am not ungenerous, Henrietta: give me time to reconcile myself to the cruel sacrifice you demand of me, I will animate myself to this act of justice. Come, clear these eyes, resume your spirits; your dejection would be a discouragement. I would feebly attempt, did I not see in your look a confidence of my success.'

'Next to Romney, you I will esteem and love.'

And we exchanged a salute.

LETTER XXVI.

I Need not, Susannah, to tell you my joy and reflections on so happy a beginning: your heart will explain them to you.

The night was far gone when the servant

servant returned from London. He brought me the following short and expressive epistle.

‘ TO MISS VERMAN.

‘ MY heart is thine; thou haſt no-"thing to fear." Seaſonably did theſe kind words come to me. I was deſpairing: they made me eaſy. I truſt to my Henrietta the happineſs of her

‘ ROMNEY.’

FEARFUL to talk of love, yet unable to ſuppreſs it from his looks, Lord Oſenvor grew ſad, penſive, and paſſed the greateſt part of the week alone in the moſt ſolitary places of Felton-Lodge. In the hours he ſpent with us he affected a mirth; and diſſipation his heart did not feel. Sometimes he would lead me ſilently to the harpſichord, then ſing what I played; but either he was out of tune, or his ſong vaniſhed into a ſigh. Often did he turn his head to hide the trickling tear, and fly from me if I happened to ſmile.

One morning he was gone abroad. We were alarmed by the ſhriekings of Mrs. Moulton, who was coming to our apartment, crying that Lord Oſenvor was wounded. We were in the firſt tranſport of our fright when his lordſhip preſented himſelf with his left-arm in a ſling, and ſome drops of blood on his coat.

‘ Be not terrified, ladies; I am not wounded: this blood is not mine; and this arm is only bruiſed.—Dear Henrietta, believe me, I am not wounded: your concern for my ſafety obliterates from my mind the danger I have ran. Sit down, I will tell you how I was attacked, and miraculouſly delivered.’

‘ Before you begin, I will ſee that arm, to be certain that this blood is not yours: you may diſguiſe your ſituation from the fear we ſhould be unhappy by knowing it. Step into that cloſet, ſuffer your valet de chambre to undreſs and inſpect whether that blood—Oh! I am in a terror!’

‘ He hath already. I am well; truſt to my honour: I would not indeed deceive you.’

‘ Be calm, Henrietta,’ ſaid Mrs. Spencer: ‘ why ſhould we doubt his word?—Deign, my lord, to gratify my curioſity: I long to know how you came by that arm, by that blood.’

So ſtrong an impreſſion that blood had made upon me, Suſannah, that, in ſpite of his lordſhip's extreme compoſure, I was ſtill diffident: his paleneſs argued for ſuſpicion; my heart hardly beat; I was obliged to call for ſalts.

‘ From me conceal your ſenſibility, Henrietta; that unfeigned intereſt weakens my reſolution; it rather indulges my paſſion than cools it. How can I deſpair of pleaſing when I cauſe ſuch an emotion in your heart! It forces a hope you will love me one day; your affliction makes me cheriſh it. Be yourſelf immediately, or I ſhall be ungenerous.’

‘ My fear friendſhip cauſed, my lord; you deſerve to inſpire it. But, pray, tell us your accident.’

His lordſhip got up, and walked a few minutes in the room to recover from his trouble; now and then his eyes upon me: ſuch loving eyes! I was ſorry I had not been able to diſſemble my concern. His countenance was more animated: he looked as if he hoped.

‘ I forget you muſt be impatient; forgive me ladies:’ and he ſat down.

‘ My reverie had carried me this morning at ſome diſtance from the park, when, turning into a little lane which leads to the publick road, I was on a ſudden aſſaulted by two ſtout fellows in ſeamens dreſſes. Before I could aſk what they wanted, one of them ſtruck me upon this arm with the butt end of a muſket. To defend myſelf would have been a folly: I delivered them my purſe, my watch, and my ring. The unconſcionable raſcals would abſolutely have all. I reſted contented with my loſs, and prepared to go, when the villain who had my watch, viewing the ſeal which hung at the chain, cried to his companion—" Jack, he is a lord; he will get us to the gallows; let us diſpatch him, ſelf-intereſt bids it." I was not a little frightened at his remark. I attempted to compromiſe for my life with the bloody-minded ruffians. I ſwore never to complain, and promiſed to convey any ſum of money they would aſk, to any retired place

‘ they

'they would fix. They went a few paces from me to consult what they should do, their muskets ready to fire, and their eyes upon me. "Trust him not, Jack; he is a lord; damned fools if we do." At this instant, I thought to be my last, a gentleman appeared some steps behind me, who, perceiving my situation, advanced with the quick undaunted steps of courage towards them with a pistol in each hand. "Villains!" One fired at him, and missed: he blew his brains out; his blood spirt up upon my coat. His fall intimidated the other, who fled, and fired in his retreat, but with the trembling hand of a coward. The report of the guns soon gathered a few men, who, following my brave deliverer, went in pursuit of the banditti. He was taken; and, when arriving upon the spot, I looked for my generous protector, found him not, he had vanished. My sorrow was extreme not to know whom I was indebted to for my life. I questioned every man who had seen him: he was an absolute stranger to them. My enquiries proving ineffectual, I took a post-chaise in the next village, where the seamen were conducted, and came here.'

WHOM would not this relation have moved? His situation between life and death, I was bathed in tears when he told it.

'What a danger you have escaped, my lord! How generous the man who saved you! That man will ever be dear to me! Never could I have been happy had I lost my friend!'

These expressions were a fuel to his flame: I could not help it. I saw in his thanks all the fire of love, and was not offended: I thought but of the life he so unexpectedly enjoyed.

'You shall no more venture abroad, my lord, unless armed or waited upon. These ruffians! I cannot think on them without horror!'

So overjoyed to hear me talk thus was Lord Osenvor, that he could not find words to shew me his gratitude; he pressed my hands, and appeared happy. No other tokens did he attempt to give me of his heart's delight: these then pleased me; I wanted no other.

A wink from Mrs. Spencer cooled my raptures; I felt that friendship or humanity had carried me too far: I began to perceive the delusion which his lordship indulged. How foolish a tender heart, Susannah! How easily it receives an impression, and over-acts it's natural feelings!

'Have you never known the charms of friendship, my lord, that you are both so amazed and delighted at the expression of mine? Do you think we have no tears to shed, no transports of joy to feel, for the person we esteem! For the sake of your peace and mind, mistake not the pleasure I have discovered at your happy escape; give it not a motive it had not: my friendship is too sincere for my having been insensible of the peril you was exposed to;'

IT was too late, Susannah; the poison had penetrated into his heart: he would not believe me. He let his passion domineer; and talked, and looked: I left the room; and, with many sighs, retreated into mine.

LETTER XXVII.

I Had not been long by myself, when Mrs. Moulton came to me.

'Here is a letter from Mr. Romney!'

'Good God! how came you by it?'

'The gardener gave it to me.'

What a flutter my soul was in!

'TO MISS HENRIETTA VERMAN.

'BY the help of gold I have discovered your retreat. This letter will safely come into the hands of my Henrietta. Of this metal never before did I know the power—did I make so noble use of it. By the help of gold I breathe the same air with Henrietta! This instant only I am fond of riches, which could procure to my soul the gratification of the sole desire it felt. I guess the reasons which hindered your dating the letter you sent me from Felton Lodge. Lord Osenvor is with you. You wrote me—" Thou hast nothing to "fear." I fear nothing, Henrietta. Of you I should be unworthy, did not I rely totally on the assurance you gave. Love, not jealousy, brought me here. A few minutes of your 'presence

'presence will compensate for the six days I have not seen you: my heart wants this comfort against the days I am still to be absent from you. A few minutes only; and then I go back to London till Henrietta will be mine. I am in the grove next to the summer-house; here, for his dear Henrietta, impatiently waits

'ROMNEY!'

'I Will go—be sure, I will go! Be not impatient; I will go!'

These words I wrote immediately, and sent by the bribed messenger.

* *

At dinner, Lord Osenvor would still continue deluded: my behaviour in the morning he still would interpret in his favour.

'You know not your heart, Henrietta; it was an enigma before you saw this arm, this blood; by these it has been unravelled. I hope, nay I am certain, no rival do I dread: will I yield to a victory which your concern has convinced me I shall obtain?'

'Is this your generosity, my lord?'

'When my hopes are founded, I am a lover; in no other character will I, or can I, talk or behave.'

I took Mrs. Spencer into the next room, and shewed her Romney's letter.

'Go, Henrietta; I will keep his lordship.'

Then through a back stair-case I joined Mrs. Moulton in a covered alley.

Love, Susannah, gave wings to my feet: in ten minutes I was in the arms of Romney. You may imagine what language we spoke; how tender the expression; how delicate the sentiment! These scenes are to be acted, not described; the pen is too cold for the fire of passion.

An hour we had forgot ourselves in the bewitching effusions of our enamoured hearts; not one thought had we of parting. He was at my feet, enjoying my smiles and my—'I love you,' when we were rouzed from this heavenly lethargy by the door being violently thrown open.

'At last I have found my rival! I can revenge myself!'

'What a fury, my lord! Is it thus you respect me?'

And I stepped between him and Romney.

'I am mad!—You shall not protect him!—Sir, defend yourself!'

'I will, my lord.'

And he turned his face to his lordship.

At his sight Lord Osenvor drew back with the greatest amazement.

'Great God! what do I see? Is it Romney who this morning saved my life?'

How I stared, Susannah!

'I did my lord: but as in the same circumstance you would venture it for me, you owe me no obligation.'

His lordship was struck dumb; he leaned against the wall, his hand before his forehead, and his eyes cast down; an awful silence reigned for a few minutes.

'How severe my fate!' exclaimed Lord Osenvor with a tone of despair; 'to be indebted for my life to the man my love had pointed out for my enemy!'

And again he sunk into a reverie.

What to do I knew not: I was so seized; I could but feel.

'Romney! why did you come to my help! why did not you let me perish by the hands of the ruffians! The life you gave I should not now detest; my death would have been so favourable to you.'

'It would not have compensated for the contempt of myself. I knew you.'

'You knew me?'

'Yes, my lord.'

'Why did you fly from me when you could have so much valued yourself upon the benefit you conferred upon me, and expect your happiness from my gratitude?'

'Could I bear, my lord, not to have been base? All men of honour would have behaved as I did. Never would you have known me for your deliverer had it not been for your coming here.'

Lord Osenvor remained sometimes pensive, totally retired in himself. I saw the dropping tears; his generosity was in arms against his passion. He advanced on a sudden towards my lover.

'Here

'Here is my hand, Romney.'

He paused, and looked at me; then, with a deep sigh—

'I will excel you in generosity! You saved my life! I yield you Henrietta! No longer do I oppose your inclination!'

And, putting Romney's hands in mine—

'Be happy! from my heart I wish you so.—Henrietta, your mother's consent I engage to obtain! Let this act of justice expiate for your wrongs!'

Susannah! I am loth to describe our emotions, our thanks: thou hast a heart, call thy fancy to it's help; paint to thyself what passed among us. Here, had fate been propitious, I would have ended these memoirs. But, alas! I was doomed to be miserable.

LETTER XXVIII.

AS we were going to the house, we met Mrs. Spencer; who, fearful of mischief, had watched and followed his lordship's steps. Our joy told her we were happy; and chaced from her features the anxiety which animated them. She stopped at some distance from us with a look of admiration, which evidently expressed—'Is it possible? you three hand in hand, all seemingly happy!'

'This is Mr. Romney, Madam, my deliverer, and your nephew.'

'Your deliverer! Oh! let me embrace the brave fellow—my nephew! —Your lordship is a man indeed! Why have not I two Henriettas? With two such men for nephews, the most insatiable ambition of an aunt ought to be satisfied.'

'By this event, charming Henrietta,' said Osenvor, with a smile, 'you have avoided a world of vexations. Your extreme sensibility in the morning had persuaded me you did not love Romney; I cherished the hope of melting your soul into tenderness; but when, after dinner, you took Mrs. Spencer apart, and did not come back, suspicion entered my heart; to despair I gave way. Under the pretext of the want of a nap, I stole into my room, charged these pistols, and went down into the garden. The pleasure of seeing one another betrayed the place of your retreat; you spoke your transports with the indiscreet voice of a real joy; it made me mad to hear; I rushed in upon you; the rest you know. Far from repenting of what I did, I will hasten the hour of your mutual happiness: it is yet early; this minute I will go to London. When from me Mrs. Verman shall learn the sincerity of your inclination, her opposition will die into the delight of making you happy.'

In vain did we all beg he would give us the remainder of the day.

'I must deserve your forgiveness and your esteem, Henrietta; I am eager to repair the troubles I have caused you.'

Mr. Romney offered to wait upon his lordship.

'No, no, Romney; you have your last sufferings to forget: stay here; to-morrow you shall hear from me; and, I dare say, from Mrs. Verman.'

The chariot was soon ready; a kiss was my farewel to him.

'Envy him not that kiss, Romney.'

'I will punish you for the apology.'

And he printed one himself upon my lips.

LETTER XXIX.

SOON my lover was the man of my aunt's fancy. The more she saw and heard him, the more she was pleased with his person and manners.

'I applaud your taste, Henrietta, in the choice of an husband; not an happier choice could you have made.'

The art of pleasing, which he naturally had, he displayed to gain her esteem. Twenty-four hours, Susannah, vanished like a dream; never breathed two more fortunate lovers. These hours of raptures were succeeded by days of horror and misery. Why, Susannah, have you bid my friendship to write what I wish I had totally forgot? My soul is torn; I doubt it will be in my power to obey. Too fiercely sad is the tale of my woe! My pen drops; this day I shall be a prey to sorrow. Tears only can I shed; I cannot write. Perhaps to-morrow—— Adieu!

I 2 LETTER

LETTER XXX.

TOWARDS the evening, we received from Mrs Verman a letter such as we would have dictated.

The certainty I loved, and Lord Ofenvor's entreaties, had forced her consent: the next Tuesday she promised to come with his lordship, and give me to Romney.

Who, after this, Susannah, would have thought I should be the most wretched of my sex? I must forget it, or I shall not proceed.

In the transports of her joy, Mrs. Spencer would that all her neighbourhood should partake of it: invitations were sent to the most genteel people for the next day.

'The interval to Tuesday must be
' passed into mirth and festivity: let us
' not perceive it, if possible.'

The nearer I draw to the catastrophe, the more inhuman is the order you gave; my heart shrinks; I have hardly life enough to hold the pen. Oh, oh, Susannah! to what trial you put my friendship for you! I cannot dwell upon the past. One attempt more I will make to please you; it may be death to me. You know not how keen the torment to write what I feel.

* *

THE company came: we danced with the spirits of overjoyed hearts. Romney—Fate had decreed I should drink of the cup of misery and despair—Romney, having over-heated himself, stepped into the next room; there he imprudently quenched his thirst with some small wine and water; it was cold. Susannah, pity me! Remit the rest of the punishment you have inflicted upon me; it is too severe; I shall sink under it!

* *

THE dances continued; when a sudden paleness on his face, and the trembling of his hand, frightened my loving, timorous soul.

' Good God! you are in a shivering
' fit, Romney!'

A fainting was his answer. I prevented his fall by opening my arms and receiving him in them. What a situation I was in! They took him from me; and I was myself carried in an elbow-chair. Doctor Herbert, who was in the assembly, felt Romney's pulse, and found him in a high fever. At that word my heart beat no more; I swooned away.

For three days I was in that state of stupidity peculiar to a mind too lively affected; I knew nobody, and had forgot Romney: Nature at last, helped by the physician, gave back to my organs the sensibility they had lost. When I could distinguish the object before me, I saw my mother and my aunt on their knees at the bed-side bedewed in tears, and lamenting mournfully their unhappy destiny.

' Where is Romney?'

It was the first words I had yet spoke.

' Thanks to the Almighty! my
' Henrietta is restored to me! She talks!
' You know me, my Henrietta.'

' I do.'

And I pressed my lips upon her hands.

' I know you, dear aunt—I know
' you too, O mother, mother! Where
' is Romney?'

Both turned their heads, sighed, were silent.

' Is Romney no more?'

' He lives still.'

' Let me see him, and then die with
' him: I shall not out-live my Rom-
' ney; the same grave will contain us
' both. I hardly breathe, deny me
' not the only pleasure which can charm
' the mortal pangs of death; it's agony
' I already feel.—Oh, Romney! how
' cruel our fate! So near to happiness,
' in one instant we fell into the abyss
' of misery.—Deprive not your daugh-
' ter of the sight of Romney; let us
' expire in one another's arms, our
' souls will take their flights together:
' such an end will be a delight.'

' Dear Henrietta, remember you are
' a Christian; that your days are not
' your own; that you will leave behind
' you the unhappiest of mothers: live
' to be the comfort of a mother who
' loves you.'

' Dear aunt, you have a tender heart;
' indulge the only wish I am able to
' form, let me see Romney. Your
' looks tell me you comply. Dear mo-
' ther, mark not with despair the last
' gasp of my life.'

' Be composed, dear girl; you shall

‘ see him when, his fever being abated, ‘ he can see and hear you: wait that ‘ moment with patience.’

‘ With patience!’

Susannah, forgive me the particulars; for the sake of Lord Osenvor forgive them to me: should he come and perceive my grief, he would be unhappy; he is my husband, I must spare him the sight of my tears, of my distress.

※ ※

In the evening Mrs. Spencer drew near me. She had no need to speak, I saw my loss in her eyes: I screamed, and sunk upon the pillow. Susannah, if you will have me live, let me draw a veil over these scenes of sadness and calamity. Adieu.

LETTER XXXI.

MRS. SPENCER, TO LADY SUSANNAH FITZROY.

MADAM,

ENTERING this morning into Lady Osenvor's closet, I surprised her on her knees, bathed in tears: her lover's name was upon her lips; three times did I hear it pronounced; as often my soul shuddered at the inexpressible sorrow marked in her accent and countenance. In my amazement I could but hear and feel her misery; I thought that time, and her husband, had erased Romney from her heart: my mistake, the calm she seemed to enjoy had caused. Poor unhappy Henrietta! she suffered inwardly; her gaiety was affected: she would deceive us, lest we should be as miserable as she. Romney she loved still, though she smiled upon Osenvor; her virtue hid from him the struggles of her heart: when he was present, she always appeared pleased and contented; probably, when by herself, thus she compensated for the continual sacrifice she made in his lordship's favour. These reflections proceeded naturally from the situation I found her in.

‘ Dear Henrietta——!’

I could say no more; and sat on a chair.

‘ Envy not Romney the tribute I ‘ pay to his memory; it is involun- ‘ tary. Lady Susannah is more inhu- ‘ man than death itself: this robbed ‘ me of my lover; she has revived the ‘ loss I made; I feel it as if new! ‘ Dear aunt, I am a wretch, whose days ‘ must be filled with an incessant keen ‘ agony! I am sick, heartily sick, of life; ‘ it is a torment to breathe as Romney's ‘ lover, and Osenvor's wife!’

This speech, uttered with the awful solemnity of despair, drew tears from my eyes, and caused a trembling in every limb. She perceived, and was frightened at the impression she had made upon me.

‘ This flight of an old passion, dear ‘ Madam, I could not possibly keep in ‘ my heart; from it, it was forced by ‘ my complying with Lady Susannah's ‘ curiosity; she would know the history ‘ of my life: I have obeyed; could I ‘ recal the past without pain? In a few ‘ days I shall recover my usual tran- ‘ quillity of mind.’

And, with a smile, she wiped the tears which flowed on my cheeks.

‘ Come, dear aunt, let us bid grief ‘ away; I will drown it in a lively tone ‘ upon my harpsichord; musick is the ‘ best physician against it. Never yet, ‘ after half an hour's playing and sing- ‘ ing, have I with indifference beheld ‘ and listened to Lord Osenvor: it seems ‘ he knows these minutes are favoura- ‘ ble to his passion; and, indeed, they ‘ soften my sufferings, and melt my ‘ soul into tenderness for him.’

I fell in with her humour, and recovered from the emotion I had felt. She played and sung with an uncommon taste and vivacity: her eyes lost their languour; and, long before she had done, she was another woman.

‘ That I may not have a relapse, dear ‘ aunt, be pleased to finish my memoirs: ‘ write to Lady Susannah, how, after ‘ having loved Romney, I became Lord ‘ Osenvor's wife. I will not think of ‘ it; I am absolutely unable to finish the ‘ task her friendship has imposed upon ‘ me.’

And she put into my hands the letters she had sent your ladyship. I promised; and in my next will keep my word. I am, Madam, your most humble servant,

S. SPENCER.

LOWER GROSVENOR STREET,
JUNE 16, 1769.

LETTER

LETTER XXXII.

MRS. SPENCER, TO LADY SUSANNAH FITZROY.

AFTER three days paſt in a continual delirium, Mr. Romney had for two hours the knowledge of himſelf: he named, called for his Henrietta, and inveighed bitterly againſt Heaven, who thus unmercifully deprived him at once of life and happineſs. Lady Bennet, affecting a fortitude none of us could aſſume, ſpoke of the vanity of human wiſhes, and reconciled him at laſt to his fate. No longer did he deſire to ſee Henrietta: 'She could not,' ſighed he, 'ſupport the ſight of her dying Romney!—Henrietta! how I love thee! And I muſt die!' He fell into a few minutes reverie; then tendering his hand to Lord Oſenvor, who leaned in a real diſtreſs againſt the bed—

'Make the tender, virtuous Henrietta, forget I have lived: would ſhe could forget it! I fear her ſorrow; at firſt it will know no bounds! Take care of her; let her live to make you happy; to be happy herſelf! The dying requeſt of a lover ſhe perhaps will not deny: ſhe loves; ſhe will comply! I muſt write, that the thought you ſhall be her huſband has charmed away all the horrors of death: ſhe eſteems you, my lord; you are worthy of her.'

His lordſhip was too much moved to anſwer with words; his tears, and an unfeigned ſorrow, told his thanks and ſenſibility.

Mr. Romney deſired to be left with Lady Bennet; and ſoon after a lawyer was ſent for. He made his will, and bequeathed to Henrietta two thouſand pounds a year, and fifteen thouſand pounds in ready-money: the remainder of his fortune he gave to Lady Bennet. He attempted to write to Henrietta; he was too weak: he recommended Lord Oſenvor and her to his aunt; and died.

I cannot deſcribe to you, Madam, the effect ſo untimely a death made upon us! What we apprehended from Henrietta's paſſion when ſhe ſhould know her Romney was no more! Lord Oſenvor looked affliction itſelf! Lady Bennet! how ſhe lamented! Mrs. Ver-man's grief exceeded ſtill ours: her Henrietta! At that moment ſhe was a real mother; her ſenſations can be felt only. Poor Mrs. Moulton! faintings and tears were her expreſſions! Never was ſeen ſuch a lively picture of perfect miſery! None durſt to enter Henrietta's room, who herſelf was then almoſt inſenſible between life and death! I took upon me to draw near her bed: my features betrayed the fatal event. Dear Madam, my heart is too oppreſſed; I muſt breathe.

※ ※

THREE times, in five weeks, Henrietta was forſaken by the phyſicians; as often an happy criſis giving a new turn to her diſtemper, reſtored her to life. In that interval, Mrs. Moulton, deſpairing of Henrietta's recovery, yielded to her mortal anxiety, and expired. We knew how fond of her Henrietta was: this new incident overwhelmed us with vexation.

Nature, at laſt, conquered the diſeaſe; my niece was ſaved. It would be too tedious and painful to paint the different ſhades of ſorrow and deſpair which for fifteen months oppreſſed Henrietta's mind and heart. During that period, we all exerted every power of reaſon and friendſhip to eaſe her of her grief: but, alas! ſhe was incapable of comfort; ſhe ſmiled only from her lips; her ſoul was dead to pleaſure. Lord Oſenvor continued his viſits; with hers he mingled his tears, and bewailed her diſaſter: his pity was unfeigned. 'Leave me,' ſaid ſhe often to him; 'leave me, my lord! Give to diſſipation theſe hours of melancholy you paſs with me. Muſt all who love me partake of my troubles, and be unhappy for my ſake? It increaſes my pain to think it is ſo! Forſake a wretch who never can know or procure any joy!' Her dejection, at the end of two years, dwindling into a tender reverie, we prevailed ſo far as to make her ſhare in the publick diverſions; at firſt with a reluctant heart; by degrees, with a viſible ſatisfaction, ſhe yielded to their charms. When Lady Bennet thought ſhe could, with tranquillity, hear of her nephew, ſhe told her the legacy he had bequeathed her, and his hope ſhe would marry Lord Oſenvor.

She ſtarted back, ſtruck with what ſhe heard.

'Do

'Do not you deceive me, Madam! Is it true he indulged that hope?'

'He did; and was going to write, to beg of you to bestow your hand on his lordship; when——'

'Stop! It was his last wish, you say?'

'It was; to me he entrusted the care of Lord Ofenvor's happiness.'

She fell on her knee; and, with both her hands clasped together, and her eyes up to Heaven—

'Romney! if thou canst hear me, smile at the sacrifice I make thee: thy last prayer I grant; Lord Ofenvor shall be my husband!'

And she arose with the looks of real content.

Unspeakable, Madam, is the pleasure we felt; it instantly communicated to every heart! What a charming scene of mirth opened in a house where talness and mourning had so long fixed their abode! Mrs. Verman, how delighted! Lord Ofenvor, who could tell his transports! A few days after, Henrietta made him happy. We all joined in thanks to the Almighty, and blessed the hour their hands were united. I am, Madam, your most humble servant,

S. SPENCER.

FINIS.

www.ingramcontent.com/pod-product-compliance
Lightning Source LLC
Chambersburg PA
CBHW020245090426
42735CB00010B/1842